PN
6519
.B8
H5
1962

D1083599

The Wisdom of the East

EDITED BY J. L. CRANMER-BYNG M.C.

BURMESE PROVERBS

Burmese Proverbs

HLA PE

John Murray

50 Albemarle Street
London

UNESCO COLLECTION OF REPRESENTATIVE WORKS—BURMESE SERIES

This book has been accepted in the Burmese Translation Series of the UNESCO Collection of Representative Works, jointly sponsored by the United Nations Educational, Scientific and Cultural Organization (UNESCO) and the Government of Burma

Printed in Great Britain
by Butler & Tanner Ltd
Frome and London

To C. W. Dunn
and H. F. Searle

The object of the Editor of this series is a very definite one. He desires above all things that these books shall be the ambassadors of good-will between East and West. He hopes that they will contribute to a fuller knowledge of the great cultural heritage of the East, for only through real understanding will the West be able to appreciate the underlying problems and aspirations of Asia today. He is confident that a deeper knowledge of the great ideals and lofty philosophy of Eastern thought will help to a revival of that true spirit of charity which neither despises nor fears the nations of another creed and colour.

J. L. CRANMER-BYNG

Contents

viii   CONTENTS

Preface

This does not purport to be an exhaustive collection of Burmese proverbs. It is intended to provide a selection of them, which can illustrate Burmese proverbial wisdom. They have therefore been arranged loosely under five headings, covering man's characteristics, behaviour, relations with others and the world he lives in. Each of these five sections is introduced by an explanatory note, and the general Introduction will, I hope, help the reader appreciate the meaning and implications of the proverbs.

The preparation of such a work in English presents many complex problems, the most formidable being the translation of Burmese rhymed sayings into idiomatic English prose, capturing the spirit of the original without sacrificing the sense: the two languages are entirely different in structure and cultural background.

Mr H. F. Searle, co-editor of the new *Burmese-English Dictionary*, encouraged me in the compilation of this book, read the manuscript and gave me wise counsel. But for his unstinted help the work might not have been completed. I am greatly indebted to John Murray for invaluable suggestions and criticisms and also deeply grateful to Mrs M. Searle, who spent many long sessions with me translating French versions of Burmese proverbs, as I have mentioned in the Introduction. U Tin Maung of the B.B.C. read the manuscript and put forward several suggestions. I have accepted gratefully many cogent comments by Mr J. Okell, who read the proofs.

I dedicate this book to my two mentors and friends, Mr C. W. Dunn and Mr H. F. Searle, who have inspired me in all my scholastic pursuits.

HLA PE

Introduction

Geographical and historical factors—political, physical, economic and human—all have a bearing on the birth of Burmese proverbs.

Burma has common frontiers with India on the west and with China (through Yunnan) on the north and north-east—two great nations which have contributed no small measure of culture and civilization to the world. To the east lies Thailand and to the south Malaya and the Indian Ocean, which has been the highway for merchants from the West since before the 5th century A.D.

The chief physical features of Burma are the thickly wooded mountains in the northern region and high wooded plateaux and hills in the east and south-east; the plains in the centre intersected by hill ridges; the Arakan Yomas, the Pegu Yomas and the Shan plateaux; and the valleys of the three main rivers—the Irrawaddy (with its tributary the Chindwin), the Sittang and the Salween—which have served as means of communication from north to south since the dawn of history. And in the south are the flat areas of the Irrawaddy delta.

The climate of Burma is mostly tropical. From May until October there is a regular and heavy rainfall; for the rest of the year there is hardly any rain. The central part of Burma is known as the Dry Zone, for here the rainfall is very light. In the hottest months the temperature in the southern and central parts of the country may be over 100° Fahrenheit, while in December, January and February the temperature may fall to 60° in the south and become progressively less in the north.

These physical and climatic conditions are mainly responsible for the distribution of both agricultural and natural products and also of the peoples throughout Burma. Burma has for as long as we know been primarily an agricultural country. Rice cultivated in wet areas as well as in the Dry Zone by means of irrigation tops the list of agricultural products. Sesamum,[1] groundnuts, cotton, maize, beans, tobacco and sugar-cane are the other chief products, all of which except sugar-cane are grown on a relatively large scale in drier areas. Rubber was introduced comparatively late. In addition, Burma has been endowed with natural resources, such as mineral oil, wolfram, tin, silver, rubies, jade; and teak forests which are mostly found in the Pegu Yomas and the south-eastern parts of Burma. Most of these exportable commodities pass through Rangoon, the principal port and capital of the country.

The indigenous races of Burma, which are of Mongoloid stock, fall into three main groups: the Tibeto-Burman, the Mon-Khmer and the Thai-Chinese. The first group is represented by the Burmese proper (concentrated especially in the Irrawaddy valley), Arakanese (along the western coastal strip), Tavoyans and Merguese (in the valleys of Tenasserim), the Nagas, Chins and Kachins and many other tribes in the mountainous regions of the north. The representatives of the second group are the Mon (in the Irrawaddy delta and the Thaton and Amherst districts), the Wa (between the Shan States and Yunnan), and Palaung (in Northern Shan States); whilst the third group includes the Shans, Karens (in Tenasserim, Karenni and the Irrawaddy delta) and Taungthu (chiefly in the Shan States). There are several thousand domiciled Indians and Chinese scattered all over Burma.

Political Setting

Politically the history of Burma down to the last decade of the 19th century can be summed up as the southward advance of Burmans, and the unification of the country at the beginning of each dynasty by powerful Burman kings, whose control was later ended by misrule or invasions from neighbouring countries. The making of Burma was periodically interrupted by the

---

[1] Sesame, annual herbaceous tropical and sub-tropical plant with seeds used as food and yielding an oil used for cooking or in salad. *O.E.D.*

struggles for supremacy between the Burmans and the representatives of the other two groups—the Mon and the Shan. Twice the kingdom of Burma came to an end through external invasion and ceased for about 60 years to exist as an independent country: the first conquest was by the Tartars in the 13th century and the second by the British in the 19th century.

Waves of migration from Central Asia had been going on for thousands of years before the Burmans descended to the plains probably in the mid-9th century.[1] Here they came into contact with the Pyus, now almost extinct, and the Mons who had already attained a high level of civilization. In the 11th century King Anawrahta (1044–77) welded into one kingdom a group of formerly independent states, and ruled them from his capital city of Pagan. Gradually he extended his sovereignty down to Tenasserim in the south and Thaton, the capital city of the Mon kingdom in the delta area; to Arakan in the west; and over the hills east of the Sittang. The city of Pagan, today one of the famous ruined cities of south-east Asia, succumbed to the onslaught of the Mongols in 1287. Burma then split up into small principalities. During the next three generations, Upper Burma formed part of the Shan hegemony with separate capitals at Sagaing, Pinya and Myinsaing (all a few miles from Mandalay), while the Mons at Pegu (north of Rangoon) held suzerainty over Lower Burma.

In 1365, the Ava dynasty was founded with its capital at Ava (south-west of Mandalay). The kings of this dynasty devoted much energy to upholding Buddhism and to encouraging Burmese literature; at the same time they tried to prevent the domination of the Shans, and attempted to conquer the Mon kingdom. Later, two kings of the Toungoo dynasty, Tabinshwehti (1531–50) and Bayinnaung (1550–81), at Toungoo and afterwards at Pegu,

[1] G. H. Luce states that the Burmans descended *en masse* into the plains of Kyaukse sometime after A.D. 835. *J.B.R.S.*, vol. XLII, pt. i, p. 80. (For a list of abbreviations and the full titles of works referred to, see pp. 108–10.)

re-established unity which lasted till A.D. 1750. The Mons then tried to wrest power again and spread their control over the Dry Zone, but they lost their gains as well as their independence for good when Alaungpaya (1752–60), Chief of Shwebo (north of Mandalay), reunited the whole of Burma. The opening of the 19th century saw the kingdom of Burma reach its widest extent; it included the whole of modern Burma together with Manipur and part of Assam. For astrological reasons or political expediency, the kings of the Alaungpaya dynasty established their capitals at Ava, Amarapura and finally at Mandalay.

Three successive wars with the British in 1824, 1852 and 1885 led to the British annexation of Arakan and Tenasserim, the delta region known as the Pegu Division, and finally of the rest of the kingdom.

After the Second World War of 1939–45, during which the country was occupied by the Japanese from 1942 to 1945, Burma regained her independence on 4 January 1948. She did not revert to the old monarchical type of government, but chose instead to become the Republic of the Union of Burma, which is at present made up of Burma proper, the Shan State, the Kachin State, the Karenni (or Kayah) State, the Karen State and the Special Division of the Chins.

Cultural Setting

Culturally Burma owes a considerable debt to its neighbours, especially to India and Ceylon. Both forms of Buddhism, the *Mahāyāna* (Greater Vehicle) and *Theravāda* (Teaching of the Elders), which came from India were in existence in Burma from the 5th century A.D. *Theravāda* Buddhism, according to the Burmese chroniclers, gained predominance over the *Mahāyāna* after the conquest of Thaton by Anawrahta in 1057.[1] And the *Theravāda*, together with its scriptures in Pali introduced

[1] So far this claim has not been supported by any archaeological or epigraphical evidence.

officially through the Mons from Ceylon, uplifted the Burmans to a plane above their kindred races. One concrete example will suffice. Burmans borrowed the Mon alphabet and reduced their language to writing some time in the early 12th century. Evangelical zeal to study and propagate Buddhism in their own language was the chief reason for this achievement. Of the members of the Tibeto–Burman sub-family, only the Tibetans and the Burmans can lay claim to a script of their own.

Burmese has a vast amount of literature: in epigraphs, on palm-leaves and folded paper, and in printed books. The epigraphical literature of over one thousand inscriptions, dedicatory in nature, dignified in style, with many allusions to incidents from Buddhist scriptures and stories, began in the early 12th century. The palm-leaf and folded paper literature of an imaginative type came into being under the auspices of Buddhist monarchs, and flourished from the 15th century until printing became prevalent in the 19th century. Its contributors were Buddhist monks or ex-monks (and also some court poetesses), and its notable features were Buddhist piety and courtly refinement of language. There was a preponderance of verse over prose. The verse literature consists of translations or adaptations of the *Jātaka* (Buddha's Birth Stories), historical ballads, panegyric odes in praise of kings, and love and nature poems, as well as epistles, letters and dramas in 'mixed style' of verse and prose. Prose literature was relatively small in amount. It comprises translations or adaptations of Buddhist scriptures and stories, chiefly the *Jātaka*, *Dhammapāda Aṭṭhakathā*, *Milinda Pañha*, *Loka Nīti*,[1] chronicles and legal precedents, the last being based mainly on Sanskrit law books. The printed literature which appeared in

---

[1] All this Buddhist literature is written in Pali and all of it has been translated into Burmese. The *Jātaka* are the 547 Birth Stories of Gotama Buddha. *Dhammapāda Aṭṭhakathā* are stories similar to those in the *Jātaka*. *Milinda Pañha* are the questions of King Milinda and *Loka Nīti* or Wordly Wisdom is an ethical treatise, much studied by Burmese Buddhists.

the 19th century covers such works as *pya-zat* (dramatized versions of Buddhist or non-Buddhist stories),[1] novels, essays and short stories.

Burmans are almost exclusively Buddhists, and Buddhism is inextricably bound up with a Burman's life. The lessons he learns from the monks, from his parents, from Burmese books and even from stage plays influence a Burman's thoughts, speech and actions. To most Burmans, Buddhism means *karma*,[2] reincarnation and *nirvana*. *Karma* can be summed up as a doctrine of 'as you sow, so shall you reap', and good or evil consequences accompany a person from one existence to another. Reincarnation will go on as long as men have desires, greed, lust, selfishness and attachment. The object in life, which is full of misery, is to attain *nirvana*, where consciousness of self ceases. This can be achieved by good living: on the positive side, by taking refuge in Buddha, *Dhamma* (the Law) and *Sangha* (the Order), by acquiring merit through charitable gifts, by pious conduct and meditation; on the negative side, by abstaining from committing sins, undertaking not to kill, not to steal, not to commit any sexual crime, not to tell lies and not to drink intoxicating liquor. Burmans are aware that Buddha is not a God: He is a teacher. His teachings are a philosophy of life, which his disciples, the monks, practise and impart to their followers. The monks are celibate and own no property. They live in monasteries, wear saffron-coloured robes, go round the village or quarter to beg food once a day, and have their meals before noon. Most Burmese Buddhists treat their parents with the reverence accorded to Buddha, *Dhamma* and *Sangha*.[3]

Many Burmans combine Buddhism with animism. Propitiation of *nat* (celestial beings and terrestrial spirits) is still carried on

[1] For the origin and development of *pya-zat* see Htin Aung's *Burmese Drama* and Hla Pe's *Konmara Pya Zat*.

[2] See also '*karma*' under the section headed 'The World'.

[3] This Triad together with Parents and Teachers are usually referred to as 'The Five Worthy Objects'.

These people take refuge in Buddhism for the sake of the world hereafter, while they propitiate, and sometimes try to placate, the *nat* for the sake of the present world. They also believe in the survival of the spirits of the dead. The numerous religious edifices and small *nat*-shrines all over Burma bear testimony to this dual faith.

A Burman is also a firm believer in magic and astrology. He often resorts to magical practices such as being tattooed and swallowing pills to achieve the power of invulnerability and other supernatural accomplishments. Astrology has been known and made use of probably by the Manipuri Brahmans at least since the 13th century.[1] It has played a very important part in the life of the people as a means of foretelling the future or of trying to avert impending danger or calamity.

The syncretic beliefs of Burmans in Buddhism, animism, magic and astrology have manifested themselves in many ways. One is the Burmans' attitude towards the white elephant. To them a white elephant is a compound of divine and sacred beings. The Buddha himself was reincarnated as a white elephant in many existences; a white elephant is also one of the seven requisites of a universal monarch; and the presence of this sacred animal brings prosperity and rain to a country suffering from drought. Besides it possesses transcendental power. It was natural for the Burmese kings to take pride in the number of these sacred animals they possessed and they were eager to assume the title of Lord of one (or more) White Elephants. History has many accounts of Burmese monarchs waging wars against other States for their possession.[2] The English saying 'That's a White Elephant' could not have originated in Burma. It is derived from Siam where the original White Elephant was also regarded as sacred, and was maintained accordingly. It was

[1] Astrology is mentioned in inscriptions of the 13th–14th centuries. See for instance *S.I.P.*, p. 155.

[2] E.g. *Hm. Yaz.*, ii, p. 364. (War between Burma and Siam in the 16th century.)

the custom of the King of Siam, when he wanted to dispose of the services of a courtier who had become obnoxious to him, to make the courtier a royal present of a white elephant. The recipient was usually ruined by the cost of the animal's maintenance.

Economic Background

Burmese people are essentially agriculturists. Rice-growing by wet or dry cultivation is the chief occupation. Ploughing, harrowing, transplanting and harvesting in orthodox ways was and still is the order of the day. The natural workmates and friends of the cultivators are tropical beasts of burden such as water-buffaloes and cattle to whom they have a sentimental attachment; and yet they look upon them as dumb animals devoid of sensitiveness. Among other domesticated animals, elephants and horses are regarded as the paraphernalia of officials, even nowadays, and the elephant is accredited with intelligence of a high degree; goats are often a symbol of shamelessness; and dogs are held to be destitute of any good qualities or redeeming features.

There have always been Burmans who earn their living or supplement their inadequate earnings by hunting or fishing, though Buddhism disapproves of these activities. Bows and arrows and spears are the chief weapons of a hunter who is often accompanied by dogs. Of the wild beasts the tiger stands for savagery and ferocity, whilst the deer stands for meekness and mildness; the monkey is noted for naughtiness; and the monitor lizard, because of its forked tongue,[1] is an embodiment of untruthfulness; its appearance is also regarded as an ill-omen, a sign of poverty.[2] Fishing with various kinds of nets and traps goes on in small streams as well as in the large rivers of Burma. Both the hunters and the fishermen, in view of their sinful

[1] Cf. *On Siamese Proverbs and Idiomatic Expressions*, p. 25.
[2] *Ibid.*, p. 31.

vocations, occupy the lowest rung in the social ladder of Buddhist Burma.

There are in Burma many kinds of manual worker and also artists and craftsmen. To list a few: boatman, raftsman, cart-driver, toddy climber (who taps the juice at the top of tall palm trees) and farm labourer; author, poet, musician, blacksmith, goldsmith, mason, sculptor, wood carver, weaver and potter.

Burmese women,[1] especially in rural areas, share the burden with their men-folk in many walks of life. They are independent, free and enjoy equal rights with the men. In marriage a Burmese wife does not take her husband's name. She can always leave her husband whenever she wishes, but divorce, a social stigma, is very rare in Burma. If such an unpleasant course has to be resorted to, the property a wife brought with her when she married is hers, and any property acquired during the marriage is divided between her and her husband. Much of the day-to-day business is in the hands of the women and they give a good account of themselves.

Social Environment

Many western writers have portrayed the Burmese people as easy-going and pleasure loving. They forget however the serious side of the life of these people who work arduously on farms and on rivers under exacting conditions. During these periods of hard work, they have scarcely any time to give attention to anything other than the task in hand. When therefore they have an opportunity to release their pent-up feelings they enjoy themselves with special fervour. Forms of amusement up to the 20th century were comparatively simple. Those that appealed most to Burmans were *pwè* (stage plays), dancing and music, playing musical instruments and singing on one hand, and on the other, gambling (usually at *pwè*), racing and boxing which they generally indulged in at the many festivals and fairs usually held

[1] See also 'Women' under the section headed 'Human Characteristics'.

at the time of the full moon; the period for such pleasures was confined to the dry season.

Burmese Proverbs

Burmese proverbs (*səgəbouŋ* means literally 'similar saying')[1] are essentially similes or parables. They are usually introduced in written or spoken language by the words 'like as' and 'as it were'. Similar in meaning to the Arabic word *maṭhal* or the Malay *upama-an*,[2] the Burmese word also embraces the ideas inherent in the Chinese words for proverb, *yen*, elegant or accomplished words, and *su-yü*, common sayings, and in the Sanskrit word *subhāsita*, well-spoken words.[3]

Səgəbouŋ are at least as old as, and almost certainly older than, the written language. Ever since Burmese was first put into writing perhaps during the early part of the 12th century A.D.,[4] they have enriched and embellished the literary as well as the every-day styles. Burmese literature, whether in prose or verse or in 'mixed style', abounds in proverbs: they formed the main ingredient of a number of literary epistles submitted to the kings of Burma by Buddhist monks.[5] Then, too, there are many collections of proverbs,[6] the most recent being *The Two Thousand Proverbs*,[7] published 1910, and *The Three Thousand Proverbs*,[8] published 1956. Many Burmans still use these sayings frequently, whether in formal speech or in daily conversation.[9]

---

[1] The term has been taken also to mean 'word picture' or 'model saying'.

[2] See *Racial Proverbs*, Introduction, pp. xv, xvii.

[3] *Op. cit.*, pp. xv, xvi, xvii.

[4] See *S.I.P.*, p. 7.

[5] E.g. *Kandaw M. Com.* and *Yazaw. K.*

[6] E.g. *Sagab. B.*, *Wisit. Link. Sagab.*, *Wisit. Por. Sagab.* and *Wisit. Sagab.*   [7] See *Sagab.*

[8] An enlarged edition of *Sagab.*

[9] See for instance the speeches of U Nu, the Burmese Prime Minister from 1947 to 1962 (except for a break in 1956 and again in 1959–60).

But many sayings which have been accepted as proverbs do not deserve the name. Some are riddles (*səgətha*),[1] others are spoonerisms (*səgəleiɳ*), and a great many are mere similes (*u'pəma*). To sift the proverbs from these other figures of speech has proved a more formidable task than had been expected. Like true proverbs, many of the pretenders are decked with rhymes and are couched in terse language, and many contain allusions to incidents from the *Jātaka* or from well-known Pali or Sanskrit works and native chronicles or are taken from incidents of every-day life. The simple tests employed to solve this problem, unsatisfactory though they are, have been (i) that the style of a proverb must be epigrammatic; and (ii) that the intention underlying the proverb is to give advice or warning or to hand on a piece of wisdom.

In trying to ascertain what a proverb is, we must look through the proverbs of many countries of south-east Asia that are adjacent to Burma, and also those of China and Japan.[2] As expected we shall notice that certain proverbs are common to two or more of these countries. In several instances some of these proverbs are almost identical both in ideas and implications; if there are differences, they are in the characters used in the proverbs. These similarities can be ascribed to three main reasons: (i) the proverbs have been derived from a common source; (ii) one of the countries has borrowed directly or indirectly from another; and (iii) the countries concerned have similar attitudes towards certain concepts.

Burma, as stated earlier, is a Buddhist land, where Sanskrit works such as the *Hitopadesa*[3] and the epics are not unknown. The Burmese proverb 'Playing a harp before a buffalo' has its counterparts in Thai, Chinese and Mon, except that the Thai has

---

[1] See 'Burmese Riddles' by Maung Wun, *J.B.R.S.*, vol. XL, pt. i, pp. 1–13.

[2] Some of these are given in *Racial Proverbs*, others in *Malay Proverbs* and *On Siamese Proverbs and Idiomatic Expressions*.

[3] 'Good Advice'—a well-known collection of ethical tales and fables.

'fiddle' for harp, the Chinese 'lute' (and 'ox' for the buffalo) and the Mon has 'zither' (and 'ox' for the buffalo).[1] This is a Buddhist way of saying 'Casting pearls before swine'. The Thai, Malay and Japanese proverb 'The teeth sometimes bite the tongue' is applied to unavoidable tiffs between friends or between husband and wife, whereas the Burmese 'Husband and wife (are like) the tongue and the teeth' obviously refers only to those between husband and wife. Greed is anathema to the Buddhists. The Burmese 'If your desire is great you obtain little' has its variants in Chinese 'He that grasps loses' and in Thai 'With over greediness one's fortune vanishes'. Ingratitude is another sin. The Burmese proverb 'Taking shelter in the shade of a tree and breaking off the branches' is echoed in the Lao 'Don't soil the tree's shade that has been hospitable to thee'. On *karma* too the Buddhist countries of Burma, China and Thailand have similar conceptions as witnessed in these following proverbs: 'A man does not lose his life if the time at which he is fated to die has not arrived' (Burma), 'If the end of his life-span has not yet come he shall not die' (Thai); and the Burmese saying 'One day to die, and one day to be born'[2] has its double in the Chinese 'There is a day to be born and a time to die'.

Sanskrit literature too has given many proverbs to the countries of south-east Asia. Sir Richard Winstedt has given a list of proverbs[3] found in Malay, Japanese and Afghan, which are derived from the Sanskrit saying: 'He who does not go out and explore all the earth is a well-frog'. To this list we may add the Burmese version 'A frog in (the puddle of) a buffalo's hoof-mark' and the Thai 'A frog in a lotus pond'. And the Malay proverb 'You can't straighten a dog's tail' has a very close affinity to the Burmese 'Threading a dog's crooked tail through a joint of bamboo'. Proverbs of many countries warn people in a similar strain to guard against 'a slip of the tongue'. The

[1] *On Siamese Proverbs and Idiomatic Expressions*, p. 134.
[2] Not included in this collection.
[3] *Malay Proverbs*, pp. 2–3.

Burmese 'If the body goes through a hole, it can be pulled out; if the mouth (tongue) slips, it cannot retract itself', the Thai 'A slip of the tongue may cause the loss of one's fortune' and the Malay 'A slip of the tongue may cause the loss of one's fortune, a slip of the foot may cause one to fall (from a tree)' are but a few of them.

It is difficult to say with certainty, whether similarity between the proverbs of two countries is due to borrowing or to coincidence. The proverbs 'Teaching a monk to read, showing a crocodile how to swim' in Burmese, and 'Teach a crocodile to swim' in Thai and Malay, meaning 'teaching a grandmother how to suck eggs', is a case in point. But in a few instances, such as the Palaung saying[1] 'People who come from hell are not afraid of hot ashes" we can say that it is a borrowing from the Burmese. And in the following examples, where the Burmese is juxtaposed with the Chinese—'In a basket it is the binding, in a man it is his clothes' and 'A man is estimated by his clothes, and a horse by his saddle'; 'Day will not break for a hen's cackle; it will break only for a cock's crow' and 'A hen does not usually announce the break of day'; and '(It is as difficult to look after) one daughter (as after) a thousand cattle' and 'When a daughter has grown up she is like smuggled salt'—the similarity can safely be attributed to coincidence.

There are also a few Burmese proverbs which are comparatively recent, and they bear so much resemblance to the English that we are tempted to consider them as imports. To cite a few: 'Silence is worth a thousand pieces (of silver)'; 'Don't look a gift ox in the mouth' and 'Because the cat's away the mice are at play'.[2]

This little book is intended to be a collection of Burmese proverbs which reflect different aspects of Burmese life. A great many of them were gleaned from prose works of the first half

[1] *Racial Proverbs*, p. 348.
[2] This is also found in the Thai, e.g. *On Siamese Proverbs and Idiomatic Expressions*, p. 22.

of the 20th century.[1] During the literary revival which followed
the introduction of the printing press to Burma in the 19th
century, many proverbs were given new currency. The various
printed collections of proverbs have been consulted and also a
manuscript collection made by Father Faure, a Roman Catholic
missionary,[2] with translations and explanations in French. From
this latter source as many suitable examples as possible have been
taken in order to give a representative selection.

As has been explained, all Burmese proverbs are terse and have
a rhythm of their own, and most of them are composed with
rhymes or jingles. Just as many English proverbs are noted for
alliteration, so are the Burmese for their rhymes.[3] To try to
capture the terseness and rhythm in translating them into
English is a near impossibility, but to reproduce the rhymes is
impossible without sacrificing the sense. Consider the following
examples—(the rhyming words or syllables are in italics):
kyɛʔhma əˋ*yo*, luhma əˋ*myo* (With fowls, the pedigree, with
men, breeding); koˊ ˋwuŋ*na* koð*a* θiˊ (Only the sufferer knows
how his belly aches); ŋojiŋyɛʔ, *lɛʔ* toˊ, (Just when he wants to
cry you touch him); and təkhuˊlaʔko *ʃa*, təliŋ*gwa*go tweˊ (He
searched for a woman whose marriage had broken down and he
found a woman who had left her husband).[4] These losses caused
by a failure to do justice in translation to the original version are
indeed great; for the effectiveness of a Burmese proverb depends
upon the sound as much as on the terseness of the wording. As
close a translation as the English idiom permits has been given,
and when the meaning or implication of a proverb is likely to be
ambiguous or obscure, an explanatory note has been added.
Where possible the corresponding English proverb is shown
by inverted commas.

[1] See the *Various Sources*, pp. 109–10.
[2] See 'Burmese Proverbs, a supplement to existing proverbs', by Kin
Maung Lat, *B.S.O.A.S.*, vol. X, pt. i, pp. 31–51.
[3] Many are in binary form.
[3] The Burmese rhyme schemes in the Proverbs are not unlike those
found in the Chinese Proverbs: see *Racial Proverbs*, p. xlii.

Proverbs express the views of men about their fellow men and about human life in its various aspects. They have been classified, therefore, under five headings: (1) Human Characteristics, (2) Human Behaviour, (3) Human Relationships, (4) the World and (5) Man. These divisions are arbitrary, and are based on convenience; a proverb may have more than one implication, depending on the circumstances in which it is used. However, each of these five sections, which consist of proverbs embodying similar ideas, is in turn divided into sub-sections. Care has been taken to group together in each sub-section proverbs that have affinities with one another. Where possible they have been arranged so as to indicate the development of their basic idea.

Human Characteristics

This section of Burmese Proverbs throws light on divers human characteristics: breed, behaviour, speech and physical features as indices to the potentialities and stupidities of human nature, and deals especially with women, who have characteristics of their own.

Burmans believe that people are like their progenitors, because 'like begets like'. This view of heredity and breed plays a very important part in shaping the life of a Burman. It is most apparent in matrimonial affairs, and especially in marriages arranged by the parents of the parties: wealth, status and other considerations all have to give way to family breeding. The first question asked by the parents about a prospective son- or daughter-in-law is invariably: 'Does he or she come of a good stock?' or 'Is there any mad person or drunkard or gambler or leper in the family?' The ancestors of the person concerned may be traced back for seven generations, because 'a gourd plant will not bear any fruit other than a gourd'. This practice is also common among the Chinese.

It is easier to go wrong in sizing up a person than in assaying a piece of gold or silver, so says an old adage. Burmans have however many touchstones by which to test a man's character. One of these is his reaction in adversity, which brings out the worst or best in a man; another is his manner of speech, since they seldom trust a suave person; the third is the shape of his forehead and of his knees; and finally his outward appearance is an index to his character. Once a man has passed the test he is worth his weight in gold and will not sink into oblivion, since 'a genuine ruby will not be scorched if tossed into the fire nor will it sink if thrown onto the mud'.

Human types cannot always be divided so neatly into the

worthy and the worthless. There is a type whose latent potentialities manifest themselves only when the right time comes. To
many Burmans everyone has a fine prospect before him, unless
he has proved himself an ignoramus. There is a consensus of
opinion about ignorance, and the futile and superfluous actions
which result from it. Lack of material wealth is preferred to lack
of intelligence. A fool is mentally blind, mentally deaf and
insensitive to all the beautiful things: 'Tell him to bring butter-
milk and he will ask: Shall I bring the jar as well?' He cannot read
the letter A even if it is written as large as a basket; above all he is,
to quote the proverb, 'a buffalo before which it would be futile
to play a harp'.[1] Many proverbs portray him as a dunderhead, a
braggart and an idiot all combined.

Burmese women have a separate place in this section. 'They
wear a skirt only three cubits long whereas a man's nether garment is twenty cubits long.'[2] In other words a man is a future
Buddha whilst a woman is not. She is characterized as being vain
and wanting to preserve her looks or enhance them when she
is elderly. Beauty is however only skin deep, since a good-
looking woman devoid of virtues is like a *butea* flower, which is
all beauty without fragrance. Able women may leave their mark
on history, but only at the expense of their domestic duties; and
a woman is likely to ruin a whole kingdom by her lack of a sense
of proportion. She is also painted as an embodiment of wiles, of
which 'there are as many as the grains of sand on nine mats'.
Nevertheless, the women of Burma have been praised for their
quick wit, their business sense, their skill in household manage-

[1] The Burmese harp today has thirteen silk strings which are attached
to a boat-shaped wooden sound-box with a long, curved neck. This
proverb has its counterparts in Chinese, Thai and Mon. See the Introduction, pp. 11–12.
[2] This refers to the *pa-hso* (nether garment) worn by Burmese men in
olden days. Nowadays men wear the *longyi*, which is only slightly wider
than a woman's skirt. The *longyi*, a cylindrical skirt reaching to the ankle,
is worn round the hips and tucked in at the waist.

ment. Thus far credit is given to them, for men claim that women's achievements are limited. Women are not therefore complementary but supplementary to men. This view is reflected in the distorting mirror of Burmese literature.

HEREDITY AND BREED

With fowls, the pedigree; with men, breeding.   [1
   'What can you expect from a man like that?' Class counts.

Naturally the same beans from the same bin.   [2
   'A chip of the old block.'

Set up a plantain, it will bear fruits of its kind.   [3

Only rivers and streams can disappear without a trace; a people cannot.   [4

Like father and grandfather alike.   [5
   'Like father, like son.'

MARKS OF CHARACTER

Only when he meets adversity will you know his character.[6
   Danger brings out the best in man.

If you want to know his origin look at his conduct.   [7
   'Manners maketh man.'

A mealy-mouthed person has an ugly disposition.   [8

Seeing the bark you know the tree; seeing his expression you know his character.   [9

When you see the water-lily stem and root you should be able to tell the depth. [10

Again this implies that outward appearance is an index to a man's character.

The mane is the proof of a real lion. [11

In a dog it's the bridge of the nose, in a cat the forehead and in a man the knee. [12

Things to look for when judging value.

The trunk is the proof of an elephant; the nose of an Indian. [13

The noses of Indians are more prominent than those of Burmans.

The soldering is proof of the goldsmith. [14

'The proof of the pudding is in the eating.'

Wax will show the quality of gold. [15

Beeswax is used for testing precious metals in Burma.

A real chilli, seven fathoms under water, will still taste hot. [16

The talents of an outstanding person can be tested anywhere.

Real ivory will not be eaten by insects. [17

A real ruby cannot sink in the mud. [18

A man of real merit cannot sink into obscurity.

If the butter is good you can serve it in a pot lid. [19

A flea's head of good medicine is enough. [20

With a basket, the binding; with a man, his clothes.   [21

'The apparel oft proclaims the man.' *Hamlet*, Act I, Scene iii.

*A lazy man lies flat on his back, a lazy woman stretches out
her legs.*   [22

PROSPECTS

Shoots grow on a pestle.   [23

Applied to a person who has achieved a success that was never
expected of him.

The chicken destined for the pot has grown fine spurs.   [24

An apparently insignificant person suddenly displaying
ability.

Steam coming out of the cold cooked rice!   [25

An ember about to blaze glows brightly.   [26

Said of a man who gives an indication of his power.

*Like one's ear, the more you look at it the farther away it
is!*   [27

A remote prospect.

FUTILITY

Playing a harp before a buffalo.   [28

'To cast pearls before swine.'

Water can never be forced into a solid bamboo.   [29

Dunderhead.

*He has not learnt anything though all the palm-leaves have
    been used up.* [30

> Oblong strips cut from palm-leaves, after being smoothed
> and polished, were in general use as writing material until
> 150 years ago. They are still used for special purposes such
> as the preparation of horoscopes.

*The silk is all used up, but Maung Pon never learned to play
    the harp.* [31

> Burmese harp-strings are made of silk and easily broken.

*You have married off all your daughters yet you haven't got a
    son-in-law.* [32

You can't get whole rice by pounding bran. [33

> 'You can't make a silk purse out of a sow's ear.'

*Though you burn a cartful of cotton-wool you won't get a hand-
    ful of ashes.* [34

> You can't expect much from a person who lacks natural
> ability.

Boil a pyi *of* thakhut *flowers, there'll be less than a handful
    left.* [35

> A variant of the last one. *Thakhut* (Bignonia) flowers have
> medicinal properties. Like spinach they boil down to
> nothing. One *pyi* = $\frac{1}{16}$ of a bushel.

If you try to sharpen a rotten bamboo it won't take a point. [36

> Cf. 'Rotten wood cannot be carved, and mud walls cannot
> be plastered.' Chinese proverb.

Digging a well on high ground. [37

> Misdirected effort.

Water falling into sand. [38

> Vain effort.

When the torrent comes he tries to dam it up with sand.   [39

Flipping sesamum seeds into an elephant's mouth.   [40

> 'A drop in the ocean.'

The moon shining in the hollow of the bamboo.   [41

> Buried talent. Applied to someone who shows off his skill and ability where they cannot be appreciated.

Giving a good dream to a dumb person.   [42

> Cf. 'Like a dumb person dreaming in his sleep.' Thai proverb. He cannot repeat the dream.

IGNORANCE AND UNENLIGHTENMENT

When the disease is not known there is no remedy.   [43

In a forest where there is no heart-wood the castor-oil plant rules.   [44

> 'Among the blind a one-eyed man is king.'

It may take an embryo Buddha to answer a buffalo-herd's question.   [45

> 'A fool may ask more questions in an hour than a wise man can answer in seven years.' A favourite retort given by those who are at a loss when confronted with a question they cannot answer.

A stupid act entails doing the work twice over.   [46

Ask when you don't know, wash when you're dirty.   [47

Those who are unaware walk over it; those who are aware unearth it and eat it.   [48

> Eyes and No-eyes. A reward awaits the observant.

*If you don't observe you won't see a cave; if you do observe you
see a speck of dust.*   [49

A jar half full of water splashes about.   [50
    Cf. 'Still water runs deep.'

He who talks isn't strong; he who's strong doesn't talk.   [51
    'Those who know don't speak; those who speak don't know.'

The blind man is not afraid of ghosts.   [52
    An ignorant person is reckless of consequences.

He rides without knowing whether it's a stallion or a mare. [53

*He gets along on his journey but he does not know the villages
on his route.*   [54
    Cf. 'The fool wanders, the wise man travels.'

Ignorance is more troublesome than poverty.   [55
    'Better to be a beggar than a fool.'

*He is told it's a crane and he asks: 'What kind of bird is
it?'*   [56

*Told that someone had been killed by a tiger, he asked: 'Had
he been ill long?'*   [57

SUPERFLUITY

*Teaching a fisherman how to knot his net or a hunter how to
spear game.*   [58
    'Teaching your grandmother to suck eggs.'

*Teaching a monk to read; showing an alligator king the water
business.*   [59

Going to China to sell needles.   [60
    'Carrying coals to Newcastle.'
    B.P.—C

WOMEN

Buttressing an old house, adorning an old woman with flowers. [61

'Mutton dressed as lamb.'

Beauty in the face, but in the body grace, and you cannot exhaust it. [62

'Beauty is skin-deep.'

She has good looks but no character. [63

'A fair woman without virtue is like pallid wine.'

Famous in history but household affairs are neglected. [64

If a woman wrecks a country it is well and truly wrecked. [65

Day will not break for a hen's cackle; it will break only for a cock's crow. [66

Cf. 'A hen does not usually announce the break of day.' Chinese proverb.

A big wave! it's under the boat; a big mountain! it's under the feet. [67

Women will always be subdued by men.

Human Behaviour

In this second section we see many and varied sides of human behaviour through the lens presented by these proverbs. The series of pictures which greets our eyes tends to be unattractive. This is deliberate; the proverbs serve as a warning and stimulate reflection on human weaknesses.

Man is egoistic, self-opinionated, self-willed. He advertises himself like the seven shameless creatures which call out their names.[1] A self-satisfied man, like a rogue, sees in another a fault as small as a sesamum seed, but in himself he does not see a fault as big as a coconut.[2] A self-willed person through obstinacy brings his own destruction upon himself. The moral is quite clear: be selfless.

Some men are comparable to a puffed-up frog, and they are often of the kind which basks in the reflected glory of others. These people are like 'a yokel employed as a footman, grinning as if the royal insignia he has to carry were his own'. Burmans regard pomposity with amusement and, whenever opportunity arises, they take great pleasure in pricking the bubble. A pompous person is often likened to the chameleon (in the *Mahosadha Jātaka*)[3] with a pennyworth of silver round its neck, which filled it with vainglory. And those who swagger about in the light of other people's achievements are also described as vultures who look like golden birds because they are perching on a golden hill!

Another is the vainglorious extrovert. An individual of this

[1] Of the seven creatures, the first is a reptile and the rest are birds. They are: the large crowing lizard or gecko, the pied crested cuckoo, the Burmese spotted owlet, the Bengal brown fish-owl, the Burmese red-wattled lapwing, the common iora and the Malay koel.

[2] *Loka Nīti Pāt Nissaya*, pp. 64–5.

[3] The *Jātaka*, vi, pp. 172–3.

species is prepared to go to any length so long as he can make a great impression on other people. He is the crow in the fable who wears peacock feathers. When such a person does a work of merit, such as alms-giving, it is likely that he will proclaim from the roof-top that he is the alms-giver! In seeking limelight to satisfy his vanity he goes on from pretension to pretension. He will live in a plank house—a dwelling that was a sign of opulence in olden days—while feeding on the cheapest kind of food, namely roselle leaves.[1] Vanity goes hand in hand with boastfulness and blustering. How often do we meet a vain person whose big talk is lacking in weight? His boasting and vaunting are cynically compared to the booming of a New Year's Day cannon.

Such people are apt to entertain great expectations and nourish high aspirations without regard to their own worth or ability, or to decorum and propriety. The proverbs in the sub-section on 'Great Expectations' show these people up as wretched beings trying to reach out for something which is not meant for them: they are like a person whose head is among the clouds, crying out for the moon. Their achievements fall far short of their expectations and their further efforts usually end in disaster like that of 'the sparrow which imitated the strut of a peacock'.

The next sub-section on 'Despair' is a grim warning to those whose aspirations have been frustrated. In such a plight and driven by despair a man may have recourse to extreme measures like the *Garuda*[2] which, having exhausted all its ideas, took to boiling salt (the occupation of the forlorn). Desperation may drive a man from bad to worse and when he finally realizes that his situation cannot deteriorate any further, he will in his desperate

[1] Roselle, the Indian sorrel. There are many varieties, but it is the red sorrel that Burmese people make use of in their everyday dishes. Both leaves and buds have a sour taste.

[2] *Garuda*, a mythical bird, half man, half bird. He is the king of birds and the greatest enemy of the *Naga* (serpents). He is usually represented as having the head, wings, talons and beak of an eagle, and the body and limbs of a man.

mood declare: 'I have become a dog and I am not afraid of excrement'.

Burmans' views on dishonesty and crookedness, with their concomitant betrayal of trust, as seen in the proverbs are most enlightening. Honesty is of course the best policy, but dishonesty should be forgiven if the end justifies it. They believe that fundamentally a man is neither honest nor dishonest; it is the question of expediency versus morality that makes him what he is. After all it is easy to be moral on £2,000 a year, but it is not easy to be moral on £200. Dishonesty is therefore an aberration, whereas crookedness, according to the proverbs, is a permanent feature which can never be altered. Believers in these proverbs of course forget the one saying: 'An error may go on for ever, but it can be set right in a moment', which is somewhat equivalent to 'It's never too late to mend'. These views have made many a Burman cautious. He is not ready to place confidence in his servants or friends, or in his wife or even in his children. He would quote Mahosadha,[1] the embryo Buddha, who said that one's secret should not be confided to anyone. The secret would be out and one would be betrayed. One of the Burmans' favourite stories of betrayal is about a wife offering a sword by the handle to the robber (with whom she has fallen in love) while he was fighting with her husband.[2] Such sweeping views have led Burmans to suspect even 'their knees'.

Dishonesty, crookedness and betrayal of trust are no doubt bad traits of human nature; but ingratitude is the worst of all. It is ten thousand times more unbearable than the winter wind. Burmans who insist that he who has had even a glass of water from a person must show his gratitude, are shocked to see an ungrateful man turning against his benefactor. He would certainly liken such a man to a dog, an animal of despicable nature. The proverbs in the subsection 'Once bitten, twice shy' have been created by men who have had bitter experiences in their lives!

[1] See the *Jātaka*, vi, p. 192.   [2] *Ibid.*, iii, pp. 145–8.

Three other kinds of human weakness are also dealt with in these proverbs: retaliation, timidity, and contempt for familiar objects. Retaliation falls into two categories. One is revenge in kind: 'A tooth for a tooth'. The other is spite: 'Unable to beat the foreigners, he pitches on the Arakanese'.[1] To the Burman Buddhists paying back in one's own coin is not the answer, for, if enmity is met with enmity, it will merely prolong the strife.[2] They will say: 'If I worsted him, some other person was bound to worst me'. Forbearance and even humility are advocated to overcome this animal-like reaction which stems from anger and spite.

The Burmese language has only one word for both timidity and cowardice. The meaning is inferred from the context or situation, or from both. Burmans maintain that to fear is human. Fear or timidity never kills a man but shame often does. Sometimes timidity has its own advantages: it keeps the timid out of trouble. On the other hand cowardice is derided. A coward is held up to ridicule, especially when he tries to keep up appearances by tackling a dangerous feat. There are many such proverbs. Courage is a different matter. A brave man 'though frightened seldom runs'. A faint-hearted man misses his chances, while a brave one attains greatness. A really valiant man can rout ten thousand soldiers.[3]

Familiarity, it is said, breeds contempt, but with the Burmans, it does more than this. Between a student and his teacher, too

[1] There are no historical records of Burmese armed forces wreaking their vengeance on the Arakanese people because they had been defeated by foreign forces. Probably this is a reference to one of the instances when ill-treatment was meted out to the Arakanese by the Burmese when they were engaged in war with the British between 1824–6.

[2] Cf. 'For not by hatred are hatreds ever quenched here in this world. By love rather are they quenched. This is an eternal law.' *Dhammapada Commentary*, pt. I, p. 174.

[3] This is a reference to the incident in which Mahosadha, the embryo Buddha, single-handed scored a victory over eighteen invading armies. See the *Jātaka*, vi, p. 206 and following.

long a contact is likely to breed disrespect on the part of the student—he may address his teacher as 'my dear brother'; between a wife and her husband, constant companionship is apt to produce apathy; and between friends familiarity often leads to one taking advantage of the other. It therefore creates in the people concerned a frame of mind that is made up of indifference, antipathy and contempt. Hence the proverb: 'When together (two people) squabble, when apart they yearn for each other'. Absence does make the heart fonder.

It may not be inappropriate to end this section with some note on old age. Burmans generally look upon an old man as physically weak and mentally set in ideas, although there are some sprightly old people who are more than a match for many a younger man in active life. Intellectually, an old man is regarded as a symbol of wisdom, experience and sound judgement. Illogical though it may sound, there are many proverbs which say: 'He (an old man) ate rice first' and 'He was born first', implying that he is more learned and mature. Most Burman Buddhists are well acquainted with the exhortation: 'Show respect to a man who is older in age, higher in status, and greater in achievements'.

EGOISM AND SELF-WILL

He doesn't see his own ill-favour, but the ill-favour of others makes him want to laugh. [68

In another's, yes, but in his own eye he sees no dirt. [69

He praises the pickling of his own fish. [70
  'To blow one's own trumpet.'

The seven vulgar creatures who announce their own names. [71
  See p. 25, footnote 1.

Crows regard no eggs but their own.   [72
  Said of people who have concern only for the interests of their
    kith and kin.

*Equate your feelings with other people's and you won't be
ill-mannered.*   [73
  'Do unto others as you would they should do unto you.'

Stabbed by one's own device.   [74
  'Hoist with his own petard.'

The tiger who courts death moves to another jungle.   [75
  One is responsible for one's own downfall.

He uncovers his own thigh and bangs it with his elbow.   [76
  'To wash dirty linen in public.'

Only the sufferer knows how his belly aches.   [77
  'No one knows like the wearer where the shoe pinches.'

REFLECTED GLORY

*Because Mr Superman is there, Mr Everyman puts out
sprouts.*   [78

He breathes through someone else's nose.   [79
  'Dress oneself with borrowed plumes.'

He leans on the white elephant and sucks sugar-cane.   [80
  Getting advantage out of one's connection with the great.

Begging for rice by showing the elephant.   [81

Like a chameleon with a pè *worth of silver round its neck.* [82
  See explanation on p. 25. A *pè* = 1/1,600 viss.

Cheeks shining because of gold earrings.   [83

A parrot is golden on a golden tree, silver on a silver tree. [84
　He takes his colour from his surroundings.

OSTENTATION

*To command respect from his neighbours he goes to the
　Government Office.*   [85
　In Burma government officials form an upper class.

*He climbs up the pole of the marquee to show his alms-
　giving.*   [86

*Mr Go-One-Better posturing with a harp without being able
　to play it.*   [87
　An impostor.

He lives in a plank house but eats roselle.   [88
　See explanation on p. 26.

The golden monastery is shining but the stomach is empty. [89
　Cf. 'Splendid without but empty within.' Thai proverb.
　　Applied to people who live ostentatiously.

A New Year's Day cannon which has no shell.   [90
　Blank ammunition is fired to announce the beginning of the
　　Burmese new year—often applied to a hollow threat or
　　boast.

GREAT EXPECTATIONS

The beef knee-bone, oh, it has no regard for the curry-pots! [91
　Said of one who makes an impudent proposal or aims above
　　his station.

A cotton dress wants to be put alongside a silk one.   [92

    Said of a person trying to claim that someone above him in status is his equal.

Wearing a blue cotton skirt she tries to reach Tawa-deintha.   [93

    Tawadeintha is the second of the six celestial abodes.

He lives in the bushes but his spirit is in the heavens.   [94

    Standing in the gutter and looking at the stars.

He stretches from a log towards the flower he cannot reach. [95

    Often applied to a man who aspires to the hand of a lady above his station.

Sparrows who emulate peacocks are likely to break a thigh. [96

    A warning to ordinary people not to be too ambitious.

With a pè *of silver he bids for a string of pearls.*   [97

He aimed at a princess and married a bazaar woman.   [98

    He falls far short of his great expectations.

Said to be marrying a captain, she married a sailor.   [99

If you take big paces you leave big spaces.   [100

    Don't aim too high lest you cannot achieve it.

A swollen idea can bring ruin.   [101

DESPAIR

When the Garuda *had exhausted his ideas he boiled salt.* [102

    He did this as a last resort, since extracting salt by evaporating brine is the most laborious and unskilled way of earning a living. On *Garuda*, see p. 26, footnote 2.

*If you have no ideas, join the Forces; if you have no rice, boil
    beans.*   [103

    No skill or talent is involved.

*Eat a section of garlic; you smell of garlic. Eat two sections;
    you smell the same.*   [104

    'As well be hanged for a sheep as a lamb.'

A broken forehead cannot be worse.   [105

    Things cannot be worse.

Someone with ringworm fears no freckles.   [106

A man turned pig no more fears filth.   [107

    The plight of a desperate person.

What is darker than midnight?   [108

HONESTY AND CROOKEDNESS

A full gut supports moral precepts.   [109

    'An empty sack cannot stand upright.'

Empty pockets, empty promises.   [110

The dishonest starve, the honest eat their fill.   [111

    'Honesty is the best policy.'

This bullock has escaped before.   [112

    It will do it again.

*It's like threading a dog's crooked tail through a joint of
    bamboo.*   [113

    'Once a crook always a crook.'

BETRAYAL AND TRUST

Maggots come out of the flesh. [114
    'Save me from my friends.'

My witness testifies on his behalf. [115

Offering a sword-hilt to a thief. [116
    'A traitor in the camp.' See explanation on p. 27.

Don't trust your knee beyond yourself. [117
    Trust no one.

Trust a slave you lose an eye; trust your children you lose both. [118

A betrayed trust is a mortal thrust. [119
    It is one's trusted friend who does it.

The blow on your back reveals the bandit. [120

Keeping a viper in your waist-pocket. [121

INGRATITUDE

Taking shelter in the shade, breaking off the branches. [122

It sleeps on leather and gnaws the edges. [123
    'To bite the hand that feeds it.'

Overturning the plate after feeding from it. [124

The monkey that I brought up tries to scare me. [125

He pays half a lime for the food he has eaten during a lifetime. [126
    Applied to a person who shows his gratitude in a very mean way.

If you stand a thin bullock on its feet it will butt you. [127

    A show of ingratitude to one's rescuer.

Turn away and he throws a stone. [128

Rescue not a two-legged being, nor try to retrieve a king's drifting boat. [129

    You may get into trouble for your pains. By 'two-legged being' is meant 'a man'.

An ungrateful person loses his way. [130

CAUTION

The sparrow was hit by a stone before. [131

    'The burnt child dreads the fire.'

Once you have died you know how to lay out (the corpse). [132

    'Experience is the mother of wisdom.'

RETALIATION AND FORBEARANCE

You break the pot, I break the bowl. [133

    'Tit for tat.'

You bite my cheek, I bite your ear. [134

A mouse has eaten my iron but a hawk has carried away your son. [135

    A villager deposited five hundred ploughshares with a friend in the town. When he came to claim them he was told that they had been eaten by mice. Sometime later the villager took his friend's son to bathe, hid him in a house, and reported to the townsman that the boy had been carried off by a hawk. See the *Jātaka*, ii, pp. 127–9.

Unable to beat the Indians he pitches on the Arakanese. [136
　　See explanation on p. 28.

Setting fire to the granary because one cannot beat the mice. [137
　　'Burn one's house to get rid of the mice.'

Throwing sand at the meat he cannot eat. [138
　　'He that cannot make sport should mar none.'

He will be ruined who tries to ruin others. [139

Enmity should not be repaid with enmity. [140
　　See explanation on p. 28.

Let enmity stop short, but love linger on. [141

*He who seeks refuge under a tree may be crushed; safer to take
　　refuge under a man.* [142
　　Men are kinder than the natural forces.

TIMIDITY AND COWARDICE

Nervous, a tiger coughs, a man shouts aloud. [143

Timidity relieves one of responsibility. [144

One dies of shame but not of fear. [145

Clenching his fist under cover of his nether garment. [146
　　See explanatory note on nether garment, p. 17.

The hero appears only when the tiger is dead. [147

*Only when the thief has run away do the tattoo spots show
　　their power.* [148
　　Some Burmans believe that tattoo marks have magical
　　power over enemy attack.

He would like to ride a difficult buffalo but hasn't enough courage. [149

The black elephant dare not look at the royal white elephant's face. [150

People of low origin have not the courage to mix with those in high position.

Faint heart misses the chance, bravery wins a throne. [151

'Faint heart never won fair lady.'

COURAGE

One can but fall to earth or rise to the golden umbrella. [152

'Nothing venture nothing win.' Earth signifies death, and the golden umbrella, kingship.

The brave don't die, or if they do, avoid hell. [153

'Cowards die often.' 'It is fear, not death, that slays.'

Although cowardly be slow to run. [154

A Samari *will not allow the loss of a hair.* [155

Samari, Pali *camara*, the Yak or Tibetan ox, is portrayed in Burmese literature as an animal which would rather lay down its life than lose one hair from its tail.

One capable man, and a force of ten thousand was crushed. [156

See explanatory note on p. 28.

FAMILIARITY AND CONTEMPT

You despise the master after a long time at school. [157

'Familiarity breeds contempt.'

Broadcast a psalm, it becomes a popular song. [158

The man from hell is not afraid of hot ashes. [159

A village ox does not feed on village grass. [160
    'The grass is green on the other side of the fence.'

Fishermen ignore the crocodile. [161

*See it often, it looks smaller; smell it often, it loses its
scent.* [162

Men ignore a barking dog. [163
    Cf. 'Barking dogs seldom bite.'

If you know the face, don't buy fish-paste. [164
    Don't do business with your friends.

AGEING

Mice cease to fear the cat when she is too old. [165

An old dog cannot be taught to sit up. [166
    'You can't teach an old dog new tricks.'

*The strongest young bullock is only as strong as an old bullock
with a broken leg.* [167

Old bullocks are partial to tender grass. [168
    Said of old men who are fond of young women.

Let the doctor be old and the lawyer be young. [169
    'An old physician and a young lawyer.'

Human Relationships

The proverbs in this section give an insight into situations that may arise between friends, relations, lovers, husbands and wives, and teachers and their pupils.

The two terms most commonly used to describe friendship in Burmese are 'comrade and ally' and 'companion since youth'. The tie between friends is very strong indeed: friends travel in the same boat, they share the same happiness and sorrows, and they go through thick and thin together. Friendship calls for sacrifice and faithfulness. Those who do not conform to these requirements are fair-weather friends. The proverbs are very harsh about such false friends. Genuine friendship, say the proverbs, also demands mutual respect, such as exists between the crow and the crow-pheasant,[1] as well as understanding and toleration; for a man has many moods.

Advice in Burmese didactic poems on the choice of friends and how to deal with them is not scarce. Burmese parents are always reminding their children of the type of person to befriend, since an undesirable companion can bring disrepute to his circle or even to his community. The contagiousness of bad habits is also stressed in proverbs of which the oldest is: 'Plant a *Khwe-dauk* (Bitter fruit) tree near a sweet mango, and the mango will certainly lose its flavour'. Once a friend is found to be false or undesirable, a Burman is often told not to break off the friendship as 'one breaks off a growing branch or a bamboo' but to do it gently.

---

[1] Crow-pheasant is as its name denotes a bird which combines the characteristics of a crow and of a pheasant. Its flight is remarkably slow. It is seldom far from water. It has a distinctive dull booming call from which it derives its Burmese name *bote*. Burmese people say that it lifts its voice only when the tide is turning. See *Birds of Burma*, pp. 274–5.

As with friends, so there are good relations and bad relations. For the self-seeking relative, there is a saying: 'He tries to establish relationship with a person only when the person has gold'.[1] The good ones are however always ready to come in time of emergency to the aid of their own kith and kin. Burmese Buddhists are aware of one of the thirty-eight principles of Buddhism: 'Render assistance to your relatives'. And there is no doubt that a too literal application of this excellent principle, without due regard to equity and justice, often leads in Burma to nepotism. All through recorded history many wealthy and influential Burmans have put this tenet into practice; and it is not rare, even today, to find a well-to-do Burman supporting a houseful of near and distant relatives: 'He is a tree which affords shelter to many travellers'.

The proverbs on relations between the sexes tend to be full of cynicism. In the East, where social contacts between men and women have not been as free and easy as they are in the West, the spectacle of frequent meetings between a young man and a girl is likely to cause a flutter in the circles within which they move, and gives rise to comments such as 'They're no saints', or remarks that such contacts are bound to end in an affair or a marriage, since 'the tip of the tongue cannot contain itself when sour fruit and salt are placed together'.[2] Many couples therefore follow the proverb 'Let the people know, but do not let them see' and have secret rendezvous, especially at night.

Married life is accepted by Burmans as a law of nature, with which they must comply. Old bachelors and spinsters are eyed with mixed feelings of pity and suspicion. Parents fear that a daughter of theirs who defies this law of nature, not 'fruiting when it is time to fruit and blossoming when it is time to blossom', may have to face the consequences: she may be left on

[1] The Burmese expression for relative is *hswe-myo* (relative-kind). Here there is a pun on the words *hswe-myo* and *shwe-myo* (gold-kind).

[2] The sight of sour fruit and salt is sure to make a Burman's mouth water.

the shelf or be led astray, or land in an ill-matched union. Marriages are of two kinds. Some come about through young people falling in love, often without the knowledge of their parents; in such cases the two lovers would either be married with the parents' blessing or, if the parents refused to give their consent, elope and set up a home as husband and wife. The other kind is arranged by the older generation. Many Burmans believe that a marriage is brought about because of the 'brow-writing.'[1] They maintain that a person who has the writing on his or her brow will marry the destined person, and that those who do not have the writing will remain unmarried.

Having gone so far as to state that marriages are made by 'brow-writing', the proverbs proceed to explain some of the reasons for seemingly ill-matched or unusual unions and for the break-up of marriages. A personable man chooses a plain Jane as his wife because he sees in her certain attractive traits. Beauty is in the eye of the beholder: if 'a Shan trader likes a bullock, it is a good-looking animal'. [2] With a couple whose disparity in age is great, the reasons are two-fold: the elder seeks a companion to lean on, the younger one to depend upon.[3] The unusual union mentioned above refers to marriages where the chief considerations are preservation of lineage, especially amongst royalty,[4] and of wealth.

---

[1] The Burmese believe that there are marks on the forehead of every man and woman which settle their matrimonial future. The idea is Hindu in origin. Most Burman Buddhists however ascribe a union to the past deeds (*karma*) of the parties concerned: hence such expressions for marriage as 'meeting of past deeds', 'joining of past deeds', etc.

[2] Shan people are noted as being the best connoisseurs of cattle.

[3] Another proverb that may explain an older man marrying a much younger girl is: 'While the (would-be) wife is still in the cradle, her (future) husband is already an ordained monk'. A man cannot be ordained until he reaches the age of twenty-one.

[4] The origin of the proverbs on marriage between members of the same family can be traced to the ancestors of Buddha. Of the nine members of the family—five sisters and four brothers—the four brothers

Most marriages, be they arranged or otherwise, last until death. These have the essential ingredients: compatibility and affection. Where they are dissolved the cause can be attributed to infidelity, and this unfaithfulness, say the proverbs, is due to a human tendency to get weary of sameness and to be attracted by novelty: 'She wears the flower when it has a sweet scent, but discards it when it has lost its scent'; 'He discards the roast fish for the fresh fish'. If matrimonial discord walks in by the front door, happiness walks out at the back.

Another cause of an unhappy marriage is the union of two spineless persons, who will never make a success of it. Such a marriage is usually abandoned in despair.

As unmarried men and women in Burmese society above a certain age are out of place, widows and widowers, divorced wives and husbands are all advised to remarry.

The proverbs about the relations between husband and wife reveal (i) the complementary natures of the two, (ii) the husband's position and his attitude towards his wife, and (iii) the wife's position and her attitude towards her husband. In spite of unavoidable tiffs between them, they realize that one is dependent on the other. A Burmese husband is in theory the master of the house, and if he so wished he could take as many wives as the minister Vidhura, the embryo Buddha.[1] Though polygamy is not illegal, it is unfavourably regarded by society in Burma, and not many husbands are prepared to be stigmatized as 'the man with a lesser wife'. On the whole a husband is kind to his wife: he does not follow the proverbial injunction not to spare a bullock or a wife. Instead he usually treats her as his sister and addresses her as such. He knows that he must not neglect or stay away from her for long—at least not longer than one month: 'Stay away one month from your wife (she may transfer her love to another); stay away from a harp three months (you will forget how to

married four of the sisters to preserve the lineage. This practice, though followed by some Burmese kings, is now taboo in Burma.

[1] Vidhura had one thousand wives. See the *Jātaka*, vi, p. 145.

play it)'. He also knows the persuasive power of her tongue, and he is resolved not to concede too much.

The wife's position, according to the proverbs, is not very enviable. In a country where marriage, building a pagoda and getting oneself tattooed are reckoned to be three things which, once done, cannot be undone, a wife seems to have the worst of both worlds. Divorce and desertion always bring discredit to her. Nevertheless, many wives prefer separation rather than suffer the agonies of living with a 'dog-like' husband.[1] A divorced woman may with propriety marry a second time, but not a third time, since that would entail social ostracism—'a woman having many faces', meaning having too many husbands or lovers.

A Burmese wife usually loves, honours and obeys her husband: 'She is his mother sometimes, his younger sister at other times and his servant the rest of the time'. In the pool of life, she regards herself as a water lily and her husband as the water: she will look well only when the water sustains her. There are of course a few proverbs which can be applied to wives who want to assert their independence. But the majority of Burmese wives look to their husbands to provide them with the blessings of this existence. For they realize that in the long run it is their husbands, and not their relatives, who are prepared to share with them what they have. A good wife is therefore willing to follow her husband through life as 'the hair knot follows the top-knot' or 'the thread follows the needle'.

The parent-child relationship in Burma is summed up in a saying that for parents 'The sight of their child is like a drop of cool, exhilarating water on them',[2] and their care stems from another maxim that the parents are the children's first teachers. The parents would always like to hear that theirs are 'true children of good parents' and they also wish them to attain the highest rung in life. Even with recalcitrant children they show

---

[1] Marriage in Burma is a social contract, and a husband or wife can dissolve the partnership by leaving his or her partner.

[2] This refers to the first coming of the rains after a period of drought.

great tolerance. The bond between parents and children is much stronger in Burma than in the West. Burmese parents like to keep their children in their home as long as they can, and to share their possessions with them. They seldom disclaim the bad ones. A few proverbs there are that misrepresent the facts, such as 'a mother will lay down her son's body and stand on it when the world is on fire', but the fact is that she would rather let her son stand on her body should such a situation arise.

Children's love and respect for their parents is a rule rather than an exception in Burma. Grown-up sons and daughters repay, in their parents' old age, the care which was given to them when they were young. They 'succour their parents, who are one of the Five Worthy Objects'.[1] Here it is significant that the good and the bad are confined to sons. The good one is likened to a precious gem and the bad one to 'a foal which wants to measure his hoof marks against his sire's'. As for the daughter, she is portrayed as neither good nor bad, except that she is a source of worry to her parents, since they are afraid that she might marry the wrong man. In reality, however, a daughter in Burma makes greater sacrifices than ten sons to comfort and solace her parents in their old age.

The tie between parents and children is paralleled by that between teachers and pupils. A teacher is revered and obeyed; he is also one of the Five Worthy Objects,[1] and as such his fame usually spreads without any advertisement. He is relied on by his pupils for knowledge and the technique of its application, as well as for moral guidance. It is natural therefore to expect that he will get credit for his pupil's achievements, and blame for his pupil's failure; but such is the way of the world, that in many cases praise goes to the pupil, and criticism to the teacher.

This faith in their teacher born of respect and uncritical acceptance of his pronouncements has made pupils in Burma meek and humble. They feel that to disown or denounce their teacher would be unpardonable, and they are obsessed by such

[1] See the Introduction, p. 6, footnote 3.

stories as that of a man whose palate was pierced by a spear[1] or of the man who was stoned,[2] when they wished to disown or vie with their teacher. Such traditions still persist in Burma.

FRIENDSHIP AND ASSOCIATION

Riding in the same boat, going on the same journey. [170

Together in happiness and trouble alike. [171

'For better or worse.'

When it is scarce, share it; when it is plentiful, take your fill. [172

'Share and share alike.'

Good times he shares; bad times he shuns. [173

Fair-weather friend.

Nga-yan *fish, he treats as joint fare;* nga-khu *fish he won't share.* [174

Nga-yan is a coarse fish, and *nga-khu* an appetising fish.

Crow-pheasant respects crow, and crow respects crow-pheasant. [175

See explanatory note on 'crow-pheasant', p. 39.

---

[1] A young man who had watched a heron throwing up fish and catching them in its beak, practised this art with a spear. He gained mastery of this technique and gave an exhibition before the king. When he was asked who his teacher had been, he replied that he learnt it unaided. At the next performance the spear pierced his palate.

[2] While the embryo Buddha was a court musician he taught a pupil of his all he knew. Later, the pupil, wishing to oust his teacher from his post, challenged him to a contest in the presence of the king. The contest was held, the pupil was defeated and stoned to death by the enraged crowd. See the *Jātaka*, ii, p. 176.

Sugar-cane is sweet always; man only sometimes.   [176

A man has many moods.

The onion by itself was all right; with chillies it got a pounding.   [177

These condiments are pounded in a mortar to make a curry dish.

The whole boat is putrid because of a single carp.   [178

Carp is a fish which goes stale quickly and contaminates the rest of a catch. The whole community's reputation suffers because of one member's misdeed.

Many crows had to perish because of one crow.   [179

One day a crow dropped filth on the king's chaplain who thereupon harboured hatred against all crows. Sometime later the king's elephant-stalls caught fire and as a result many elephants were badly burnt. When the chaplain was consulted, he said the cure for burns was crow's fat. Many crows were accordingly slaughtered for their fat. See the *Jātaka*, i, pp. 300–1.

Near a fisherman one is a fisherman; near a hunter a hunter.   [180

'A man is known by the company he keeps.'

Ox to ox, novice to novice.   [181

Keep indigo and madder together; the madder will smell of indigo.   [182

Bad habits are contagious.

Virtue and morality keep similar company.   [183

'Birds of a feather flock together.'

Minds together, bodies apart. [184

Have dealings with a person but keep yourself away from
him.

If long, persist; if short, cut off. [185

Associate with an even-tempered person, have nothing to do
with a short-tempered one.

If the cattle are scattered the tiger seizes them. [186

'Unity is strength.'

RELATIVES

He calls her aunt only when her cucumber fruits. [187

A real friend is a relative, a dish you like is a feast. [188

'A good friend is my nearest relative.'

In time of test, family is best. [189

'Blood is thicker than water.'

*When the sister prospers the brother rides high; when the
brother prospers the sister is in the kitchen.* [190

A good tree can lodge ten thousand birds. [191

INEVITABILITY

*Pot against pot, the pots will touch; ropes together, the ropes
will tangle.* [192

Constant contact between a boy and a girl leads to love.

*Place sour fruit and salt together, the tip of the tongue cannot
contain itself.*   [193

> Two people of opposite sex cannot help attracting one
> another.

MARRIAGE

Fruit in autumn, blossom in spring.   [194

> 'He that marries late, marries ill.'

The brow-writing gets around the villages.   [195

> 'Marriage is destiny.' See the explanatory note, p. 41.

*A bullock is handsome if a Shan likes it; a bed is a palace if
you fancy it.*   [196

> 'Beauty is in the eye of the beholder.' The Shan people are
> great cattle-fanciers.

Take a fancy to a toddy-palm leaf, to you it's a fairy.   [197

> Marry the person one fancies.

Young enough to be carried; old enough to depend upon.   [198

> See the explanation, p. 41.

If it is to be spent, let it go into one's own pocket.   [199

> A justification for marrying a rich relative.

*Take cover among relations, you are secure; marry a relative,
you are blessed.*   [200

> Advising a union between relatives for security and pre-
> servation of lineage. See the explanation, p. 41.

*Like minds, happy for life; unlike minds, always out of
mind.*   [201

Forget not for a century youth's beloved; forget not for a hundred centuries youth's companion. [202

First love.

At the sight of fresh fish away goes the roast. [203

Said of unfaithful wife or husband.

Hot in the front rooms, not cool in the back. [204

Strain in matrimony affects children as well as domestic staff.

Guests only come to a happy house. [205

Happy atmosphere in the house.

Hacking a bamboo with a blunt knife. [206

Said of two weaklings marrying one another.

A hare-lipped couple blowing up the fire. [207

A tree falls, plant another. [208

A favourite saying with widowers and widows who want to re-marry.

MARRIED LIFE

(Like) tongue and teeth. [209

Tiffs are inevitable between husband and wife.

Grass depends on the island, the island on the grass. [210

Interdependent.

Take a wife, the cat must die. [211

The husband kills the cat to show his wife his mettle.

Do not spare a bullock or a wife.   [212

'A spaniel, a woman, a walnut tree, the more they are beaten the better they be.'

The wax hardens when it's away from the fire.   [213

Advice not to leave one's wife for long.

Hard to know what to eat; hard to know where to keep a wife.   [214

The dilemma of a jealous husband.

If you love your wife, praise her only when she is dead.   [215

After saying it many times she prevails.   [216

She gets her way by nagging.

Side with a woman, side with foolishness.   [217

If the thorn falls the leaf is pierced; if the leaf falls the leaf is pierced.   [218

'Heads I win, tails you lose.' The worst of both worlds. The plight of a wife.

Loss of goods is one day spoiled; loss of a husband is a ruined life.   [219

Don't have a dog for a husband.   [220

Three times the monk has changed monastery, three times the woman her husband.   [221

They are ostracized by the public.

Only at high water is the water-lily at its best.   [222

The wife's position depends upon her husband's.

A handful from a good friend, a basket from a rich relative— but from a good husband a happy life.   [223

PARENT AND CHILD

Parents are the first teachers (of the children).   [224

Bad children? Blame the parents.   [225

They'd like to see him riding an elephant, surrounded by horses; not trampled by elephants and kicked by horses.   [226

Discard only bad baskets and punnets, not bad sons and daughters.   [227

With the world afire a mother will lay her son down and stand on his body.   [228

When in agony a mother will even deny being related to her son.   [229

A heifer is not attached to her calf.   [230

A mother is not attached to her first child.

What foolishness over the first child!   [231

The womb remembers and calls him 'son'; the money paid brands him 'slave'.   [232

If you listen to your parent's words, you can boil slabs of iron and stones and they will become soft.   [233

Feeding is reciprocated by feeding, tending by tending.   [234

Children should repay their debt to their parents in the latter's old age.

One worthy son, one valuable gem.   [235

Both are difficult to get.

One in a thousand mothers bears such sons.   [236

A foal measuring his hoof-marks against his sire's. [237
> Said of a son who defies his father.

If possible he would dig for treasure on his father's forehead. [238
> Unfilial conduct.

The care of one daughter equals that of a thousand cattle. [239

A motherless son is a fish in low water. [240

TEACHER AND TAUGHT

A real master needs no flag-staff. [241
> 'Good wine needs no bush.'

Even roasting fish-paste calls for a teacher's guidance. [242

A bad pupil? Blame the teacher. [243

Praise goes to the pupil, detraction to the master. [244

Treat a pupil kindly, he will break your heart. [245

Because he vied with his teacher he had bricks thrown at him. [246
> See footnote 2, p. 45.

The pupil's skill is less than his master's. [247
> A variation of the above.

Try to surpass your teacher, you become mad; try to surpass your pony, you become giddy. [248

The World

The world has an omnipresent force called *karma*,[1] which presupposes a belief in reincarnation. *Karma*, literally meaning deeds, is indefinable, but can be described as the sum total of the actions that make up one's life or the accumulation of merits and demerits in past existences as well as in the present existence. All Burmese Buddhists believe in it and it pervades all the aspects of a Burmese Buddhist's life. The popular concepts of this word are varied and a Burman acts or behaves in the light of his own understanding of it.

Generally speaking there are two main schools: the first accepts *karma* as the arbiter of life. It is equated to fate and the attitude towards it is one of resignation. The protagonists of this school feel that they are mere children in the hand of *karma*, which determines their life or death, their wealth or poverty, their health or sickness and their happiness or sorrow; and that its rewards and punishments cannot be foretold. *Karma* therefore is a supreme and unpredictable authority, since 'one can see a man carrying on his shoulder a spear but not *karma*' (good or bad luck). This certainly sounds like Micawberism, but it is manifested in many a Burman's not infrequent remark, 'It's *karma*', when something has gone amiss, or in his behaviour when seemingly he is preparing for the worst and hoping for the best.

The second school maintains that *karma* is what we make of it. If it means 'deeds', then deeds can be modified by the doer. Their views as expounded in several proverbs are: Rely not solely on your *karma*; do not risk yourself by having a blind faith in *karma*; accept it but place not yourself at its mercy; exercise your intelligence as well as your assiduity in battling against the vicissitudes of life.

[1] See the Introduction, p. 6.

The vicissitudes of life—prosperity and poverty, success and failure, fame and obscurity, as echoed in the proverbs are the inevitable laws of life. None of these has a permanent control over men. Since *karma* has a hand, a man may be rich one day and poor the next. Neither will the great be perching for ever on the top nor will the lowly one be always struggling at the bottom: every dog has his day. Failure is as much a phase as success. Many Burmans console themselves in their hour of dire distress with the fate of Mahosadha, the embryo Buddha, who temporarily lost his status of a Minister and had to earn his living as a potter.[1] This philosophy of mutability has made most Burmans what they are: contented, carefree and proud.

The presence of *karma* is felt by Burmans in every sphere of their lives. The world is full of unexpected and inexplicable phenomena and incidents. One is coincidence which can be at once pleasant or unpleasant. Many of the proverbs about it have one important moral: Don't trust circumstantial evidence, the arrival of a person may coincide with the disappearance of a bullock, but it can, all the same, be a mere fortuitous accident. Further, a person may score a great success in an undertaking, but it can equally be a fluke.

Other such phenomena and incidents are those which afford delight or cause disillusionment and disappointment. The proverbs poignantly illustrate that the world is a bed of roses as well as of thorns. Who is more delighted than the thief who is appointed to the trusteeship of a treasury—though in a few cases he himself became a reformed character and rose to a high rank?[2] To counter-balance this there are instances in which a man who has been holding someone in high esteem finds out that that person has feet of clay; or in which a person revering something that he thought was a pagoda discovers that it is only an ant hill when he sees a monitor lizard[3] running out of it.

[1] See the *Jātaka*, *vi*, p. 186.
[2] See *Hm. Yaz.*, i, p. 440.
[3] See explanation of 'monitor lizard' in the Introduction, p. 8.

The rest of such imponderables are incongruities, paradoxes, untoward incidents, dilemmas and quandaries. The proverbs about these have Burmese wit and humour and many of them are rather caustic. Incongruities are chiefly found in absurd relations, misguided or mistaken actions and ill-assorted elements. A man has to pay more for the accessories than for the main item; he 'tucks up his nether garment' (a preparation that is meant for a strenuous task) 'to catch a winkle'; and 'useless things are often perceived among valuable objects'. To the Burmans, as to the British, it is paradoxical to put the cart before the horse or to count one's chickens before they are hatched; but one thing that is peculiar to the Burmans is that 'a son can never be older than his father', that is a father is assumed to be more knowledgeable than his son, because 'he ate the rice before his son did' (that is, he is older and wiser).

The world is topsy-turvy; that is what the proverbs say. Untoward incidents and the least expected things happen to people. A person desiring merit pours water on a sacred banyan tree[1] and 'is put instead to the job of carrying the drums' (a form of punishment in olden days). On the other hand some one breaks the branch of a sacred banyan tree and he gets a pot of gold. This cynical saying has given birth to many which though popularly used are not taken seriously. A few of these are: 'Drinking liquor will lead to *Nirvāna*' (Immortality) and 'Eating opium will win the love of one's wife'.

The world is not only imperfect, but also tantalizing as well as aggravating. There are many occasions on which people have been placed on the horns of a dilemma or in a quandary, and in many instances they simply fall between two stools. A man who by chance 'gets hold of a tiger's tail' has an unenviable choice of two unfavourable courses—either to let it go or hold on. Another man, like the one who has a piece of juicy meat that is

[1] Banyan trees are looked upon as sacred by Burmese Buddhists because the last Buddha attained enlightenment under a banyan tree (*Ficus religiosa*).

covered with grit, will have to study anxiously to avoid a disagreeable outcome. Equally unhappy is the man who tries to catch two fish and loses both.

Aggravation is of two kinds: one makes the people worse off and the other adds insult to injury. People who are dissatisfied with their life, often yearn for a change, expecting an improvement. When it comes, more often than not it brings contrary results which they have not bargained for. The proverb 'The old monk clouted the monastery boys only once, but the new monk clouts them twice' illustrates not only this point but also it gives insight into the mind of a Burman: he is suspicious of the new order. The saying has been used every time a new ruler or government has turned out to be worse than the old one. In some cases a person in peril looks for help from the quarter where he expected to get it, but the would-be rescuer proves to be more dangerous than the peril. There are many proverbs to show that misfortune never comes singly and that fortune smiles on the favoured and frowns upon the unlucky. Many Burmese Buddhists accept these mischances with equanimity as their lot, while others blame the world for such inequities.

The proverbs have so far projected an image of the world in an unfavourable light: it has more faults than virtues. Nevertheless those headed 'The Biter Bit' prove that the world seldom lets the unscrupulous and immoral go scot free. A biter is usually bitten in the end. A smart individual is bound to meet his match ultimately. *Karma*, whether taken in the sense of a dynamic or a static force, seems to have a hand in all the affairs of the world.

KARMA

Karma is the mother and karma *is the father.* [249

    Karma is supreme.

A man does not lose his life if the time at which he is fated to die has not arrived. [250

    'He that is born to be hanged shall never be drowned.'

He will be poor, however intelligent he may be, if he has no karma. [251

If the gale of karma *blows a mountain of rock will be blown away.* [252

Wherever the damsel of ill-fortune goes there the rain follows. [253

    One cannot escape one's *karma.*

When circumstances are favourable water will flow up-hill. [254

The future price will be fixed in the future; sell it at the current price. [255

    Let the future look after itself.

The mouth chiselled by a divine being and not by a human being. [256

    If a mortar made by human hands gets rice from time to time, a human mouth made by divine power is worthy of a regular supply of food.

A lucky tiger! While it's running it finds a deer. [257

At the proper time the thin ox will kick. [258

    'Wait and see.'

Sawkè became king without aspiring to it.   [259

    Sawkè, a distant relative, was compelled by circumstances to
    accept the throne when the king died. See *Hm. Yaz.*, i,
    p. 442.

A worthless man blames his karma.   [260

    'A bad workman blames his tools.'

*Do not tread on a heap of thorns because you have faith in
your* karma.   [261

*Where there are bold tigers about you are not justified in
blaming your fate.*   [262

    Don't take unnecessary risks by relying too much on your
    karma.

Karma *watches over your property; your intelligence watches
over your life.*   [263

VICISSITUDES

Sometimes poor, sometimes rich.   [264

Strong currents one moment, slack water the next.   [265

    Hard time and easy time.

The top of a pinnacle now, fire-wood soon.   [266

First the hare was ahead and then the hound.   [267

One day the stump is higher, next day it's the grass.   [268

    'Every dog has his day.'

I will wait inside the bush and sharpen my horns.   [269

    I'll strike when my turn comes.

Waiting in the sun for the shade to come. [270

'There is no summer without winter.'

COINCIDENCE

Just as you arrived my bullock disappeared. [271

Just as the palm-nut fell the crow stepped on it. [272

Just when he wants to cry you touch him. [273

Give him a pretext for doing what he wants to do.

A blind fowl came upon the rice-pot. [274

It's a fluke.

Just when the egg-plant is thin the knife is blunt. [275

Said of a difficult situation which arises just when one is
powerless to deal with it. When an egg-plant shrivels its
skin becomes very tough and cannot easily be cut.

DELIGHT

A thirsty man falls into a well. [276

Sending to Toungoo a person who is fond of betel-nut. [277

'Fate gives a helping hand.' Toungoo, a town in Burma,
abounds in betel-nut palms.

Dropping the Cula tortoise in the water. [278

A council of ministers discussed the severest form of punishment which could be imposed upon the Cula tortoise and
at the suggestion of a stupid minister it was dropped into
the river Yamunā. See the *Jātaka*, vi, p. 83.

Letting an alligator loose in the water. [279

To hold an old dog on a leash. [280

As you are fated to eat (honey), bees swarm in your beard. [281

Appointing a thief to a trusteeship; employing a witch to roast meat. [282

'He sets the fox to keep the geese.'

Going with a package and parcel to a place where there are thieves. [283

He searches for a woman who has been divorced and he finds a woman who has divorced her husband. [284

DISILLUSIONMENT

I have worn pinchbeck mistaking it for gold! [285

A man finds out that a person he had been holding in high esteem has feet of clay.

Thinking that it was a relic of the Buddha we put it on a stand and worshipped it. Only when it was actually on the stand did we realize that it was a kalein *seed.* [286

'*Kalein* seed' is a Molucca bean.

Supposing that it was a pagoda I adored it; only when a monitor lizard ran out did I realize that it was an ant-hill! [287

I gave him (my daughter) in marriage thinking that he was a chettyar; *only at dawn did I realize that he was a lay-brother.* [288

Both the *chettyar* and the lay-brother have shaven heads and wear white clothes; but *chettyars* are bankers from South India and lay-brothers are mendicants.

Just as I was praising my daughter's discretion, out she came ride-a-cock-horse on the wooden spoon. [289

She let her parent down.

He was all right while he was sitting; only when he got up did I realize he was lame. [290

He showed himself up by doing something that he ought not to.

Why! he claims to be the consecrator of the five-storied monastery; in fact he's merely a tout for the monk from there! [291

INCONGRUITY

The price of the hook (goad) is greater than the price of the elephant. [292

The accessories cost more than the main item.

A pè of merit, a viss of hell (sin). [293

On *pè* and viss, see No. 82.

As the chicken was ill he consulted an astrologer and was told to sacrifice a buffalo. [294

Using an iron bar to crack a boiled egg. [295

'To break a butterfly on the wheel.'

Attaching a mouse's ears to a hog. [296

Ill-matched.

A monk has no concern with a comb. [297

Because he has a shaven head.

The loin-cloth is tucked up where there are no buttocks. [298

    Barking up the wrong tree.

He chops at one place and it is cut at another. [299

The bank at Nyaung U collapsed and the cow at Sampa-nago got a broken back! [300

    Said of people who are affected by events far removed from them.

San Pa (a man) claims to have been shoved about by the crowd although he has not been to the public show. [301

A lame man trying to climb toddy palms is out of place. [302

    An incompetent person taking on a formidable task.

Putting goods on the royal barge. [303

    The royal barge was an enormous boat of state, in which the king usually made his journeys on the river.

Gilding and bedecking with gems the oven-bricks. [304

When diamonds are being sold, the tobacco-stalk merchant is in the way. [305

    Worthless people meddling in serious business.

The lame dog gets in the way of a good steed as it runs along. [306

Rat droppings mixed with rice-offerings. [307

    Useless stuff among valuable objects.

His mouth says: 'Buddha, Buddha', but his hand acts contrari-wise. [308

    A fake.

Travelling by raft and yet thirsty. [309

Going to plough and forgetting the cattle.   [310

The desire to laugh is stronger than the desire to weep.   [311
  A misfortune that arouses laughter rather than sympathy.

PARADOX

The son is one month older than his father.   [312
  A son is trying to be cleverer than his father.

The harrow sticks out in front of the bullock.   [313
  Often said to impertinent young people.

The monkey chasing the owner of a hillside farm.   [314
  Fox chases hounds.

The thief cries: 'Man! Man!'   [315

He goes to bed last, yet falls asleep first.   [316

The frog that is roasted last is cooked first.   [317

She was born last, yet she wants to be called Miss First. [318
  Said of people who act out of their turn.

*Before he becomes proficient in the goldsmith's art he learns
  how to steal gold.*   [319
  'He tries to walk before he can crawl.'

He has stretched his legs before he's sat down.   [320

Searching for a lime before he gets the hare.   [321
  'Putting the cart before the horse.'

*Wanting to return to the secular life before you have been
  initiated (into the Order).*   [322

*Your mouth is already sticky before you have the chance to
    taste the soup.*   [323

   'Counting one's chickens before they are hatched.'

Yearning for his aunt rather than his mother.   [324

He who has no pa-hso *says: 'Sit so that you do not show your
    legs.'*   [325

   'The pot calling the kettle black.' See note on *pa-hso*, p. 17.

The horseman who asks for help from the pedestrian.   [326

*You humbly apologize to him only after you have slapped his
    head.*   [327

   'Apology after insult.'

Looking for a pupil he finds a teacher.   [328

Looking for a good blanket he found a phalan *tree.*   [329

   A very coarse cloth is obtained from the bark of *phalan*
    trees.

He was at Meza without having been exiled.   [330

   Meza was a penal settlement in north Burma.

UNTOWARD INCIDENTS

*Desiring benefit, I poured banyan-water, but caught the job of
    carrying the drums.*   [331

   Applied to the penalty brought on oneself from helping
    others.

His thigh was broken because he planted a bodhi *tree.*   [332

   The Bodhi is a sacred banyan tree. See the explanatory note
    on the sacred banyan tree, p. 55.

He secured a pot of gold because he broke (the branch of) a (sacred) banyan tree.   [333

Because he wanted to become airborne he had the figure of a cat tattooed on him; but the ink merely added to his weight. [334

Said of something which is more of a liability than an asset.

Wanting to have delectable food I joined an orchestra, but had to pay five rupees because I trod on an oboe.   [335

Exposing in the sun a person who likes to be cool.   [336

Because the wild ox tossed him he arrived on the bush.   [337

Blessing in disguise.

DILEMMA AND QUANDARY

Like one who by chance has taken hold of a tiger's tail: afraid either to hold on or to let go.   [338

'Between the devil and the deep sea.' Cf. 'He who rides a tiger can't dismount.' Chinese proverb.

Padaing fruit, if squeezed in the hand, pricks you; if eaten, makes you mad.   [339

'To be on the horns of a dilemma.'

If you push forward you meet the yoke; if you draw backwards you hit the cross-beam of the cart.   [340

As to eating it, well, it is covered with grit; but as to throwing it away, well, it is rich and luscious.   [341

I have no money to pay (the debt) and no land to abscond to. [342

When I work for my living the rains are scanty; when I steal for my living the dogs bark.   [343

He fails to find his rich uncle and in the meantime he misses the festival of putting the umbrella on a pagoda as well. [344

'To fall between two stools.'

He does not catch the monitor lizard and he has lost his chopper. [345

The oar broke while the boat was going well. [346

His successful notes were spoilt by the noise of 'Ding-dong'. [347

When a lunatic, who was pointing out where treasures were buried, realized that people were taking down notes, he distracted their attention by shouting 'Ding-dong'.

WORSE OFF

The old monk clouted once, but the new monk clouts twice. [348

Maung Pa Lè, the newcomer, is worse than the Minister of Shields. [349

'Better the devil you know than the devil you don't know.'

Only with a new ruler do you realize the value of the old. [350

Woe to the river when a monitor lizard becomes an alligator. [351

In Burmese folklore the monitor lizard, which has a tongue and so a sense of taste and can enjoy its food, is able to turn itself into an alligator; whereas a crocodile has no tongue and eats only to fill its belly. Usually applied to men of low birth occupying high positions. Once they have a taste of power they will stop at nothing and those under them often suffer.

*Being afraid of the tiger he takes refuge with the Lord Spirit,
but the Lord Spirit is worse than the tiger.* [352

> 'Like the flounder, out of the frying-pan into the fire.' *Shin-gyi*,
> lit. 'Lord Spirit', is one of the terrestrial supernatural beings
> whom many Burmans propitiate.

AGGRAVATION

Sore upon sore. [353

> 'Misfortunes never come alone.'

With the world afire the oil-lamp blazes up too! [354

Eczema comes on the leprous place. [355

While being troubled by snakes, he is harassed by centipedes. [356

*Adding a pumpkin when it's already weighed down by a
gourd.* [357

> 'Double, double toil and trouble'. Both gourd and pumpkin
> plants fruit on a frame. When the frame is already weighed
> down by gourds it has to bear the weight of pumpkins as
> well.

The ash-chariot has arrived for the monitor lizard prince. [358

> Poverty upon poverty. For Burmans the colours of both
> monitor lizard and ashes denote poverty. The *Jātaka*
> stories relate that in ancient India, when a kingdom was
> left without a king, ministers would send out into the
> streets a driverless ritual chariot. It would wander through
> the streets and stop eventually in front of the future king.
> The term 'ash-chariot' used here is a play on this custom.

Probationers being few he tried to recruit novices; but then the lay-brother reverted to being a layman.   [359

'It never rains but it pours.'

The breeze rises where something is on fire.   [360

'To bring oil to the fire.'

Serving a cold man with water, setting fire to a hot man. [361

'To add insult to injury.'

The thief pounds you when you have fallen.   [362

Driving a spear into low ground.   [363

The down-trodden usually gets trodden on.

Pushing a drowning man still further down with a bamboo. [364

'Pour not water on a drowned mouse.'

Water! it flows to low ground.   [365

Don't kick a man when he is down.

Pieces of curry-meat go to the man of high position.   [366

The poor get only the gravy.

Enriching the rich man.   [367

A variant of the preceeding one.

I owned that I was frightened, yet he touched me with a cat.   [368

Told to buy sugar-cane and suck it, he bought and ate sweet potatoes.   [369

Sugar-cane cleans one's teeth, but a sweet potato dirties them; hence he brings trouble upon himself.

THE BITER BIT

When one smart individual meets another he has his neck severed. [370

'When Greek meets Greek, then comes the tug of war.'
A crafty crane living near a pond where the water dried up
in summer offered to carry the fish to another pond where
water was plentiful. The fish agreed and one by one they
were taken and eaten by the crane, till only a crab was left.
The wily crab agreed to go, but he clung round the crane's
neck while being carried along and severed the crane's
head with his pincers when he discovered the crane's
intention. See the *Jātaka*, i, p. 95.

To tonsure a bald head. [371

A Russell's viper bitten by a snake. [372

The sneak wrests it from the thief's hand. [373

Man

The proverbs in this section, which is a sequel to the previous one on 'The World', are concerned with men. Some of these reveal various aspects of man's life and others show men the way to adjust themselves to their surroundings in the form of grim warnings and pieces of cogent advice.

Men toil throughout their life in a vain endeavour 'to fill nine inches of belly' and 'to cover eighteen inches of back'. The average and the mediocre can just make both ends meet, while the wretched and spendthrift go on 'fetching water in an open wicker basket', and the able and intelligent accumulate wealth. Nevertheless, the proverbs will have it, all these men are not really happy: 'those who have money are worried about it, and those who do not have it, long for it'.

Wealth and poverty, which are frequently identified with success and failure, are often the outcome of men's actions. 'Living in a suitable place, having acquired good *karma*, observing moral conduct and possessing virtuous friends', says a Buddhist axiom, are the requirements for success. The proverbs however assert that thrift, seizing an opportunity, swift action and perseverance are the ingredients. Thrift is not merely saving money, it is wise spending, and not 'penny wise, pound foolish'. Opportunity comes only once and unless 'a man stores up the water (especially in Upper Burma) while it rains' he is likely to find himself in a predicament in time of need. Many people not only miss an opportunity; they are sometimes caught unprepared like the man who 'sharpens his arrows only when the battle begins'. Dilatoriness, like procrastination, is the thief of time. Instead of taking opportunity by the forelock, many men dawdle and let the chance pass by. Burmans have a pungent saying about such people: they are 'like a bull which (instead of taking on the other bull) merely answers nature's call and sharpens its horns'. To ensure success in any undertaking constant application is essential and to do things by halves is inconceivable to a resolute man whose motto is 'One must be as slow and steady as a Palaung,[1] if one wishes to eat the best pickled tea-leaves'. Perseverance is a compound of industry and patience. Many well-disciplined Burmans realize that one's industry is not rewarded immediately, especially if it involves hard labour. Their precept and practice in such matters is 'Clear water cannot be obtained from a well that has just been dug'.

Some Burmans like to entertain great expectations and to set about trying to reach their object without any plan, and others sit and wait for it to come. The proverbs about such men are all condemnatory. 'He reads writings on treasure-trove hoping to find it', or he sits and watches as 'a paddy-bird watches a water-outlet'.

People from the West have described the Burmans as being too polite and consequently not speaking their minds. There is some substance of truth in this; but there is some reason for such behaviour, namely tactfulness. If a Burman 'wants flesh he asks for bone',[2] and he generally sets his sail as the wind blows and acts according to the circumstances. This is of course a piece of hypocrisy to westerners who are not acquainted with Burmese orthodox teachings and homilies which lay stress on not offending other people unnecessarily. 'Terminological inexactitudes' are permissible if the means justifies the end, and Burmans will seldom look upon a person, who uses blunt tactics, as a man of good breeding.

The proverbs advocate that a Burman's action shall match his tact. Appropriateness is the keynote of his daily actions. Where a bradawl is called for to execute a fine piece of work, a chisel is

[1] Palaungs, a tribe in north-east Burma, are expert tea growers.

[2] Another version is: 'He asks for liver because he wants flesh'. It is a reference to the story in which a man wanted to get a piece of meat from a hunter, and he got it by asking the hunter to give him a bone.

out of place. He is also reminded by the proverbs that as many a valuable word is wasted on the wrong ear, many a good deed is wasted on an unappreciative man, since 'the marrow of a lion is too fine for an earthenware dish; it will stay only in a cup of the finest gold'.[1] And a Burman can adapt himself to his environment and acts as Rome does when he is in Rome: 'When he slips he joins the circle of sitting people'. Those who are not certain of the accepted standard of behaviour are advised by the proverbs to conform to the popular wish. 'Do as others do when the heavens collapse': this is a piece of advice as well as a consolation given to those who expect exceptional troubles.

Prudence, according to the proverbs, should be one of the guiding principles in one's speech and actions. It is the antithesis of indiscretion and excess. Discretion and caution are implicit in these proverbs. One mouthful of unsuitable food, one imprudent step and one indiscreet word can endanger one's life. One cannot be too cautious in what one does. 'The teeth that are to chew for a long time must avoid bones' sums it up very well. Indiscreet words too are to be eschewed; but if a man has to use them 'when he speaks at night, let him look below,[2] when in the day let him look behind', to ascertain if there is anyone about. The proverbs are quite explicit that to carry tales is unforgivable, to keep silence is golden, and to answer 'No' to all kinds of enquiries leads to a happy life. This is the Burmese counterpart of 'See no evil, hear no evil, speak no evil'.

An enemy of prudence is excess, which is one of the deadly sins. Follow the middle way, says the Buddha. 'Adjust the strings of the harp so that they are neither loose nor taut', and only then will melody be achieved. Immoderation in love, excess in knowledge, in industry and in generosity—all these have disastrous effects; and the consequences of intemperance in dressing, speak-

[1] This saying is derived from 'Give ear and hearken, as if you were filling a tube of gold with lion's marrow'. The *Jātaka*, i, p. 4.

[2] In olden days almost all Burmese houses were built on stilts, the floor being at least four to five feet from the ground.

ing, spending and sleeping, a few of man's daily activities, are indeed many times worse. There is a sharp reminder to the Burmans that too much of a good thing can also be a bad thing. Too many doctors and too many tasty ingedients in the cooking pot often produce the least expected results. As for avarice, which is a form of desiring too much, the Burmese proverbs are in line with the Chinese and Siamese in censuring it. Greed together with anger and ignorance is the root cause of all the evils of this world—so says Buddhism.

If there are undisciplined Burmans, it will not be for lack of proverbs on discipline and responsibility. Freedom without these two spells chaos. A floor which has no binding[1] defeats its own purpose. To enforce discipline, authority and order is necessary so long as the world of men is imperfect. Otherwise mice will be at play if the cat is away and the jungle cat will rub his paws with glee if the jungle is on fire. Those in authority too need to set a good example, for 'if the abbot climbs up the balustrade', says one trenchant proverb, 'the novice will go one better by climbing onto the shelf above the oven'.

A wag once said: 'Trifles make perfection but perfection is no trifle'. Perhaps he had in mind the Burmese stock expression 'Never mind', when he was indulging in this witticism! Burmans, through force of habit or casualness, use the expression even when the matter is far from trivial. Many Burmese proverbs insist that trivial things can give rise to serious consequences. Even one drop of honey was once responsible for the destruction of a whole kingdom.[2] Conversely, some proverbs maintain that there are trivial things which can be safely ignored. These are of course persons, actions or things of no consequence such as a dog's flea, 'a pinch of sparrow's excrement' and 'a bullock clapper'.

The proverbs slate meddlesome individuals, and they censure

[1] The Burmese floors in olden days were made of split bamboo tied together at the side of the house.
[2] See the story, *J.B.R.S.*, Vol. v, pt. i, p. 23.

the people who practise passive neutrality. To the busybodies the exhortation is 'Don't concern yourselves with things "as the Elephant Minister's lady does",[1] which are no business of yours: neither should you worry unnecessarily about other people'. To those at the other extreme, the neutralists, the warning is that they will not incur resentment but misfortune and catastrophe. A small state between two powerful warring states may be crushed for no fault of its own like 'the *myeza* grass[2] between two fighting buffaloes'. In some cases a person suffers the same plight as 'the matting of the granary wall does' when the chicken pecks it in trying to get at the paddy. This is the way of the world.

ECONOMICS

Nine inches of belly is an ocean. [374

Neither the stomach nor the ocean can ever be filled.

Fail to work one day and be hungry for a month. [375

The water that the Indian fetches is not sufficient for his own use. [376

Living beyond one's income.

Ten rich householders will not be able to make enough contributions to support one poor household. [377

It is the kitchen that makes away with one's property. [378

As the water flows so is the dam raised. [379

As the husband earns money the wife saves it.

[1] An Elephant Minister's wife saw a *must* elephant and was worried lest its penis might hit a tree-stump. *B.E.D.*, i, p. 30.
[2] This is a common grass, probably *Cynodon dactylon* Pers.

Picking up frogs with a perforated bag. [380

An industrious husband and a spendthrift wife.

As the doe gives birth to a fawn the tiger eats it. [381

It is difficult to make both ends meet.

Half a bushel is spoilt for one anna's worth. [382

'To lose the ship for a halfpennyworth of tar.'

With an eye for a spoonful the whole pot is ruined. [383

'Penny wise, pound foolish.'

The prospect of getting a white elephant is cancelled by the receipt of a single (white) cotton thread. [384

A Burman usually refuses to accept a small gift or offer if he has an expectation of a bigger one.

(Adjust) burden to strength, like arrow to bow. [385

'Cut the coat according to the cloth.'

When you incur a debt the king will settle it. [386

Eat, drink and be merry. The attitude of a spendthrift.

He who has, worries; he who has not, longs. [387

'To have money is a fear, not to have it a grief.'

The bigger the tiger the bigger the pug-marks. [388

The more money a person gets the more expenses he incurs.

Though the centipede has one of its legs broken, this does not affect its movement. [389

A small financial loss has no effect on a rich man.

When an elephant shrinks it's still a buffalo. [390

A wealthy man in reduced circumstances will still be as well off as a well-to-do person.

MAKESHIFT

Looking for a squirrel until one gets a bird. [391

'Somewhat is better than nothing.'

Until timber is available, use bamboo as a girder. [392

OPPORTUNITY

Store up the water while it rains. [393

'Strike while the iron is hot.'

Draw the thread while the moon shines. [394

'Make hay while the sun shines.'

He cast the net only when the fish had gone off. [395

It is too late to grieve when the chance is gone.

Putting the fowl on its perch at daybreak; spreading out the paddy at sunset. [396

Shutting the stable door after the steed is stolen.

While we wait for the rain the plants in the nursery-plot wither. [397

'Procrastination is the thief of time.'

Setting sail only after the village has been passed. [398

Arrows all gone before the battle begins. [399

Sharpening your arrows only when the battle begins. [400

Doing a thing at the eleventh hour.

Looking for a tree only when the elephant chases you. [401

A stupid man conceives an idea only after the event. [402

DILATORINESS

You busy yourself with mending the rowlock, and lo! you have arrived at Ywathitkyi (Big New Village). [403

Applied to a person who takes an unnecessarily long time to get ready.

Dropping dung and sharpening his horns—that's all the big red bull does. [404

He never fights.

A boat-load of broad beans is cooked before His Majesty is ready to come out. [405

Often said of a lady who takes a long time getting ready to go out.

PERSEVERANCE AND PATIENCE

If you dive down, go on till you reach the sand; if you can climb up, go on till you reach the top. [406

'Never do things by halves.'

One day, six feet; where will Pagan move to? [407

'Slow and steady wins the race.' The idea is that even if a boat-man only progresses up the river six feet each day the city of Pagan will still be in the same place, i.e. slowly and surely will get you there in the end.

Let not the hand which has been wetted get dry. [408]

Once a work is started do it till it is finished.

He's only just dug a well and he wants to drink clear water at once. [409]

'Rome was not built in a day.'

Only just married and she wants to give birth to a child. [410]

EXPECTANCY

He dropped a fish-hook wherever the fish sent up bubbles (expecting to catch it). [411]

A man who expects to make a success of something without thinking it out.

Expecting to have ripe fruit to eat as one climbs to the top. [412]

A paddy bird watching a water outlet. [413]

Mr Micawber.

He cleared away the bush because he saw a hare. [414]

'An axe to grind.' Applied to people who undertake something with an ulterior motive.

One only gets the smell of frying, one doesn't get any fried fish. [415]

Cf. 'Jam tomorrow, but never jam today.'

I didn't know that my mother-in-law was going to die! If I had I would have bought a horse to ride. [416]

A person who would have been less cautious had he known that a fortune was awaiting him.

TACT

To ask for a bone if one wants flesh. [417

Watch the direction of the wind and set sail. [418
  'As the wind blows you must set your sail.'

The verse will halt if the tongue's too true. [419
  Painters and poets have leave to lie. Often used to justify
  exaggeration in speech.

He starts chiselling the moment he appears. [420
  Said of a tactless person who employs blunt tactics.

Overcome violence only by gentle means. [421
  'A soft answer turneth away wrath.'

Only if one accepts suffering will one enjoy benefit. [422
  'No pains, no gains.'

APPROPRIATENESS

Bore with a bradawl, chisel with a chisel. [423
  Where gentle means are called for violence is out of place and
  vice versa.

If a needle can pierce it don't chop with an axe. [424
  'Don't take a hammer to crack a nut.'

*Tie a chicken with an elephant rope, it will slip off; tie an
elephant with a chicken-tether, it will break.* [425
  Applying the wrong kind of discipline to a person.

The pea-hen sits on the sparrow's eggs and vice versa.   [426

> Applied to a head-strong leader with weak followers and a
> weak leader with head-strong followers.

*You can't catch a minnow with a wide-mesh net, nor catch a
shark with a piece of muslin.*   [427

> Adjusting means and ends.

You can only hold lion's marrow in a pure gold cup.   [428

> See p. 72, footnote 1.

In the Garuda *country be a* Garuda; *in the* Naga *country
be a* Naga   [429

> 'While in Rome do as Rome does.' See notes on *Garuda* and
> *Naga*, p. 26.

You are skilled at what you are familiar with.   [430

> 'Every man to his trade.'

MAJORITY

Drink the bitter rain-water as others do.   [431

> Conform oneself to the popular wish. A royal chaplain told
> the king that bitter rain containing impurities would fall on
> a certain day and that whoever drank it would become
> insane. The rain fell as foretold and all the people in the
> kingdom, except these two, drank it and became insane.
> But the chaplain and the king finding themselves in the
> minority had to drink it in the end.

Do as others do when the heavens collapse.   [432

Buddha found it impossible to go against the strength of the
Order.   [433

The wish of the majority usually prevails.

If the fire is greater the fire wins; if the water is greater the
water wins.   [434

PRUDENCE

When your strength is not sufficient, humble yourself.   [435

'Discretion is the better part of valour.'

If a sane dog fights a mad dog, it's the sane dog's ear that is
bitten off.   [436

'He that toucheth pitch shall be defiled therewith.'

One mouthful of unsuitable food, one imprudent step may lead
to peril.   [437

'Look before you leap.'

The teeth that are going to chew for a long time should try to
avoid bones.   [438

Husband your resources.

Though you would like to beat the dog, you have to consider
its master's face as well.   [439

One must consider various factors to avoid an imprudent step.

Even if you do not love him (her), hold your breath and kiss
him (her); even if you do not kiss him (her), heave a
sigh.   [440

The anger of the prudent never shows.   [441

Let them know about it but not see it. [442

    An advice not to commit an indiscretion publicly.

One can't go to bed when a visitor stays late. [443

Seven days is the length of a guest's life. [444

    Don't outstay your hospitality.

Visit not without invitation, eat not what does not suit you. [445

*When you speak at night look below, when you speak in the day
look behind.* [446

    See explanation on p. 72.

Let the words spoken in the jungle disappear in the jungle. [447

    'All that is said in the kitchen should not be heard in the hall.'

Silence is worth a thousand pieces (of silver). [448

    'Silence is golden.'

*If you carry the word 'NO' with you, you will never be poor
even in old age.* [449

*If the body goes through a hole it can be pulled out; if the mouth
slips it cannot retract.* [450

    'Better the foot slip than the tongue.'

EXCESS

Tune the harp strings to be neither too loose nor too taut. [451

    Follow the middle way.

Moderation is medicine, excess is peril. [452

    Moderation in all things.

The more violent the love, the more violent the anger. [453

    Cf. 'Love me little, love me long.'

Excessive knowledge leads to renunciation, excessive industry to distraction, excessive favour to passion. [454

Excess in clothes leads to debt, in spending to slavery, in eating to harm, in sleep to stupidity. [455

    'Every extremity is a fault.'

Commit yourself in speech, you become a slave. [456

    'Let not your tongue cut your throat.'

The kind-hearted becomes a slave. [457

The good-hearted has a heavy load. [458

    People will take advantage of you.

Too many doctors and the son dies. [459

    'Too many cooks spoil the broth.'

Too much carp makes the curry insipid. [460

    Too much of a good thing. The Rohita carp is one of the best fish.

Too much talk will include errors. [461

Words! Utter many and they will reveal your breed. [462

He who deliberates too much ruins his cause. [643

    'He who hesitates is lost.'

Teasing eventually turns to a quarrel. [464

A stumpy dog wants to quarrel, a stumpy man is short-tempered, a stumpy boat is difficult to steer. [465

AVARICE

Great desire obtains little. [466

    Grasp all lose all.

A needle comes in and an axe goes out. [467

    Large loss for small gain.

Because he would not eat it, the food got maggoty. [468

    Said of close-fisted people who are too mean to put their possessions to good use.

The greedy man! His words are sweet. [469

DISCIPLINE AND RESPONSIBILITY

A floor which has no binding is in disorder. [470

    See p. 73, footnote 1.

A skein of yarn which has no binding (to keep the thread in place). [471

Because the cat's away the mice are at play. [472

When the jungle is on fire the jungle cat slaps his arms. [473

    Lawless elements take advantage of lawlessness. Slapping one's arms signifies glee or triumph.

If the monk climbs up the balustrade, won't a novice climb onto the shelf above the oven? [474

    Most Burmans do their cooking on a wood fire, and above the fire-place is a shelf on which are placed things that need drying by smoke and heat.

Rain-water leaks through the roof-top. [475

    People high in the hierarchy set a bad example.

TRIFLING AND TRIVIAL

Starting from the rubbish, it burnt the pyathat *(a mansion).* [476
  'Dangerous fire begins in the bed straw.'

The country is destroyed for a drop of honey. [477
  See explanation on p. 73.

Trifling! trifling! the nose bleeds in the end. [478

Drowning in shallow water. [479
  Said of a person whose failure or downfall is due to a minor
    mishap.

The cat walks by but the dewdrops don't fall. [480
  An action of no consequence has no effect on serious matters.

Dust does not rise because a dog-flea hops. [481

The dog may bark but the ant-hill will not run away. [482
  'The dog barks but the caravan goes on.'

A pinch of sparrow's dung cannot serve as manure. [483
  'One swallow does not make a summer.'

One sesamum seed will not make oil. [484
  Sesamum oil is popularly used in Burma for cooking. See
    explanatory note on sesamum, p. 2.

*Although the bullock-clapper claps, it will not give sesamum
  seeds.* [485

UNNECESSARY CONCERN

There's nothing the Elephant Minister's lady need worry about. [486

See note, p. 74.

Although the pot's not hot the lid is. [487

Said of people who are unnecessarily worried about others.

The tethering post shook but not the pony. [488

The bush is worried on the hare's account. [489

It's not the sticky rice that is sticking, but the rough rice. [490

The person concerned in a matter does not mind but an outsider does.

NEUTRALITY

Mye-za grass between fighting buffaloes cannot survive. [491

The plight of a weak neutral state between two powerful warring states. See note on *mye-za* grass, p. 74.

The matting suffers because the chicken eat paddy. [492

See explanation on p. 74.

When the log was struck by lightning, the chameleon was hit too. [493

Said of a third party who suffers in a war or quarrel.

A bamboo growing between two trees. [494

If the hill topples, the grass is uprooted. [495

    Applied to the plight of dependants when they lose their chief
    supporter.

Contracting malaria while collecting alms. [496

    Incurring blame while carrying on one's daily task.

Key to Pronunciation

The symbols employed for the representation of Burmese sounds are the same as those used in the new *Burmese–English Dictionary*, now being issued in parts by the School of Oriental and African Studies. The system is as follows:

Vowels

ɑ in open syllables, p*a*lm; elsewhere the same sound shortened.

i in open syllables, *ea*ger; elsewhere p*i*n.

u in open syllables, *too*; elsewhere p*u*t.

e Fr. *élève*.

ɛ in open syllables. Fr. *élève*; elsewhere w*e*ll.

ɔ l*aw*.

o Fr. *eau*.

ei *ei*ght.

ou b*o*lt.

ɑu d*ow*n, s*ou*nd.

ɑi f*i*ne.

ə *a*bove.

Consonants

b, d, g (as in *go*), h, j, k, l, m, n, ny (as *gn* in Fr. *digne*), p, r, s, t, w, y (as in *you*), z approximately as in English; but aspiration of k, s, t, and p must be avoided.

c an intimate combination of *t* and *y*, resembling the initial consonantal sound in *tulip* or the *ch* of *cheese* made with tip of tongue touching lower teeth.

ŋ when initial as *ng* in *singer*; when final, a nasalization of the preceding vowel.

θ *th*in.

ð *th*en.

ʃ *sh*ake (no rounding of lips).

88

h following a consonant indicates aspiration of that consonant, as in
   kh, sh, th, ph, ch. Preceding a consonant, it indicates that that
   consonant is a breathed consonant; thus *ŋ, n, m, l* are voiced
   consonants while *hŋ, hn, hm, hl* are breathed consonants—*hl*
   being = the *ll* in *Llandudno*.

ʔ is a glottal stop as in the Cockney or the Glasgow pronunciation
   of *water* as waʔer. For convenience this is further dealt with under
   Tones.

Note.—Assimilation of final nasals before certain consonants is not
indicated in the phonetic transcription, e.g. `*paŋna* 'asthma', and
`*paŋdaiŋ* 'winning-post', which should be pronounced `*pan na* and
`*pan daiŋ*.

Tones

The term 'tone' is here used to describe four of the five categories of
sound found in Burmese, the fifth, the neutral *ə* (as in *a*bove) being
regarded as non-tonal.

The *level* tone.—A syllable in this tone is low-pitched relatively to
adjacent syllables. No fall of pitch is permissible but it can rise towards
the end. Lightly stressed in comparison with syllables in other tones
belonging to the same combination. Level tones are left unmarked in the
phonetic transcription, as *sauŋ* 'blanket'.

The *heavy falling* tone.—This is high-pitched at the start and falls
steeply. Pronounced in a 'breathy' voice ending in a 'fade-out'. Heavily
stressed. Marked by ` preceding the syllable, as `*sauŋ* 'harp'.

The *creaky* tone.—Pronounced with an intermittent voice, falling
from a relatively high initial pitch and ending in a weak closure of the
glottis. Marked by ' following the syllable, as *sauŋ'* 'to wait'.

The *abrupt* tone.—Rather higher in pitch than the creaky tone.
Terminates in a glottal stop produced by an abrupt closure of the glottis.
Accompanied by much greater effort and constriction of the larynx than
the creaky tone. Marked by ʔ following the syllable as *sauʔ* 'to be steep'.

Burmese Texts

1. cɛˀhma ə`yo luhma ə`myo
2. ði pouˀ`thɛga´ ði `pɛ thwɛˀhma`bɛ
3. hŋə`pyɔbiŋ saiˀ mi´laiˀ pha´ba
4. `chauŋ`yo `myauŋ`yoða teiŋ`gɔdɛ lu`myo məteiŋ`gɔ
5. ba´ `myo `bo tu
6. ə`ciŋ əcaˀko twe´hma´ əle´ əciŋ`go θi´ya´dɛ
7. zati´go θi´jiŋyiŋ əmu əciŋ`go ci´
8. ə`pyɔ choyiŋ θə`bɔ o
9. ə`pwe myiŋ əpiŋ θi´ ə`θwe myiŋ əθwiŋ θi´
10. ca`yo cazwɛgo myiŋ yedeiŋ yenɛˀ θi´ya´mɛ
11. chiŋðe´ hmaŋ məhmaŋ hmiŋzaŋ θɛˀθe
12. `khwehma hnəyauŋ cauŋhma nə`phu luhma `du
13. shiŋ houˀ`cauŋ hnə`mauŋ θɛˀθe kə`la houˀ`cauŋ
    hnə`khauŋ θɛˀθe
14. bədeiŋ taˀ mətaˀ gəhezaˀ θɛˀθe
15. ʃwe ə`cauŋ phə`yauŋ θɛˀθe
16. ŋəyouˀ`θi hmaŋ khuŋnəlaŋ ye ŋouˀ `sa saˀtɛ
17. shiŋzwɛ hmaŋ `po mə`sa`bu
18. bədə`mya hmaŋ nuŋ məniˀ
19. `thɔbaˀ `kauŋ sə`lauŋnɛ´ thɛ´
20. `she `kauŋyiŋ `θaŋ`gauŋ
21. `tauŋ əkuˀ lu əwuˀ
22. yauˀ`ca `pyiŋ `cɔ `khiŋ `meiŋma´ `pyiŋ chi `shiŋ
23. jəbwe´ ətɛˀ pauˀ
24. `hiŋ `sajɛˀ ətɛˀ`kauŋ pauˀ
25. thə`miŋ`jaŋga´ əŋwe´ thwɛˀ
26. tauˀ chiŋdɛ´ `mi`gɛ əʃeiŋnɛ´ `yɛ`yɛ
27. ci´le `wele nəywɛˀlo

28. ˋcwɛˋba ˋsauŋ ˋti
29. ˋwa nəˋbiŋgo ye ˋθwiŋlo' məwiŋ
30. pe kouŋywe' sa məca'
31. ˋpoða kouŋlo' mauŋ pouŋ ˋsauŋ mətaʔ
32. θəˋmi kouŋywe' θəmɛʔ məya'
33. ˋphwɛgo ˋthauŋywe' shaŋˋgauŋ məya'
34. waˋguŋ təˋhlɛgo phouʔywe' təshouʔ məya'
35. θəkhuʔpwiŋ'go dəbyi pyouʔywe' təshouʔ məya'
36. wəˋshwego chuŋywe' məthɛʔ
37. ˋkouŋ khauŋgauŋhma yeˋdwiŋ ˋtu
38. ˋθɛˋdɛ ye ca'
39. ˋchauŋye la ˋθɛ kaŋˋðiŋnɛ' ˋshi
40. shiŋ'pəzaʔ ˋhnaŋ pɛʔ
41. wəˋlouŋˋgauŋˋdɛ la' θa
42. lu a' eiʔmɛʔˋkauŋ ˋpe
43. əna məθi' ˋshe məʃi'
44. əhniʔ məʃi'dɛ' ˋtɔ cɛʔshubiŋ ˋmiŋ mu
45. əˋme ˋcwɛˋjauŋ əphye phəˋyaˋlauŋ
46. məleiŋma hnəkha ˋmɔ
47. məθi'yiŋ ˋme məsiŋyiŋ ˋshe
48. məθi'ðu cɔˋðwa θi'ðu phɔ ˋsa
49. gəyu' məmu gu məmyiŋ gəyu' mu myu myiŋ
50. məpye'ði' ˋo bauŋbiŋ khaʔ
51. luˋbyɔ məθaŋ luðaŋ məˋpyɔ
52. myɛʔsiˋˋgaŋ təshe məcauʔ
53. ˋmyiŋ ˋsilo' əˋthi əma'ˋhmaŋ məθi'
54. khəˋyi twiŋlo' ywaziŋ məθi'
55. məʃi'dadɛʔ məθi'da khɛʔ
56. ˋjoja sho bɛhŋɛʔˋlɛ ˋme
57. ˋca kaiʔlo' θebadɛsho na taʃeˋla ˋme
58. təŋago paiʔ ˋtho θiŋ mouʔˋshogo ˋθa ˋtho θiŋ
59. ˋphouŋˋji sa cha' mi'ˋjauŋˋmiŋ yeˋgiŋ pya'

60. təyouʔ pye aʔ ˈyauŋ ˈθwa
61. eiŋ o ˈca kaŋ ˈmeiŋmaˈ o ˈpaŋ paŋ
62. hlaˈ təmyɛʔhna yiŋ dəgoˈlouŋ ˈθouŋyweˈ məkouŋ
63. əˈshiŋ ʃiˈ əˈchiŋ məʃiˈ
64. yazəwiŋ pyauŋ eiŋdauŋhmuˈ liʔlaʔtɛ
65. ˈmeiŋmaˈ phyɛʔ pye pyɛʔ
66. cɛʔmaˈ tuŋloˈ ˈmo məˈliŋ cɛʔphaˈ tuŋhmaˈ ˈmo ˈliŋ
67. ˈhlaiŋ ˈci hle auʔ tauŋ ˈci phəˈwa auʔ
68. ko məhlaˈ ko məmyiŋ θu məhlaˈ ŋa yijiŋ
69. koˈ myɛʔˈchi ko məmyiŋ θuˈ myɛʔˈchi ŋa myiŋ
70. koˈ ŋəchiŋ ko chiŋ
71. koˈko ko phɔ məθudə khuŋnəˈpa
72. ˈciˈgaŋˈmyolo koˈ uˈhmaˈ ko hmaʔtɛ
73. koˈ seiʔnɛˈ ˈhnaiŋ məˈyaiŋ
74. koˈ ətaʔnɛˈ ko ˈsu
75. θejiŋdɛˈ ˈca ˈtɔ ˈpyauŋ
76. koˈ pauŋ ko hlaŋ ˈthauŋ
77. koˈ ˈwuŋna koða θiˈ
78. ŋəˈkɛ ʃiˈywe ŋətiˈ ənyuŋˈ pauʔ
79. θuˈmya hnəˈkhauŋnɛˈ əθɛʔ ʃu
80. shiŋbyudə hmiˈbi caŋ souʔ
81. shiŋ pyaˈ shaŋ ˈtauŋ
82. ŋwe dəˈbɛ lɛhma ˈshwɛyaˈdɛˈ pouʔθiŋ
83. ʃwe nəˈdauŋyauŋjauŋˈ ˈpa pyauŋ
84. ʃwebiŋ ˈna ʃwe ˈce ŋwebiŋ ˈna ŋwe ˈce
85. eiŋˈniˈjiŋ yoðeauŋ ˈyouŋ tɛʔ
86. əhluʃiŋˈhmaŋ θiˈauŋ ˈmaŋdaʔtaiŋ tɛʔ
87. məphyiʔˈphɛnɛˈ θaˈgɛ ˈsauŋ təwiŋˈwiŋˈ
88. nedəˈ pyiŋdauŋ ˈsadə chiŋbauŋ
89. ʃweˈjauŋ pyauŋbyauŋ ˈwuŋ khauŋgauŋ
90. əshaŋ məʃiˈdɛˈ θəjaŋ əmyauʔ
91. əˈmɛ ˈduˈyohnɛ ˈhiŋ ˈohmaˈ ˈa məna

92. chipə`shoga' `po pauŋjiŋ
93. chibya thəmeiŋnɛ' wədeiŋ `hlaŋ
94. lu ne chouŋ`ja sei? ne bouŋ`bya
95. məhmidɛ'`paŋ `touŋ khu'lo' `hlaŋ
96. `dauŋ tu'lo' saθəŋɛ `hlaŋ che`hlaŋ cɛ pauŋ pɛ'
97. ŋwe də`bɛnɛ' pə`lɛ`gouŋ shaiŋ
98. `nyadə' `zeðɛ ywɛdə' məhanwɛ
99. cədə' hleθə`ji `nyadə' hle`do`ða
100. ə`hlaŋ cɛdə' əlɛ la?
101. əcaŋ `cidə' pyɛ?`siyataiŋ
102. əcaŋ kouŋ gəlouŋ `sha chɛ?
103. əcaŋ məʃi' `yɛ lou? shaŋ məʃi' `pɛ pyou?
104. dədɛ? `sa cɛ? θuŋ hnətɛ? `sa cɛ?θuŋ
105. pau?`pyidɛ' nə`phu mə`thudə`byi
106. `pwe əpye'`ða `tiŋdei? `swɛhma məcau?
107. wɛ? phyi?`pyidɛ'nau? məsiŋ məcau?tə'`bu
108. ðəgauŋdɛ? nyiŋ' mənɛ?tə'`bu
109. uma' tauŋ'hma' θila' sauŋ'
110. ou?sa məʃi' gədi' məti
111. kau?θə mə`salau? phyauŋ'ðə `sa məkouŋ
112. chaŋ khouŋ`budɛ' `nwa
113. `khwe `migau? cidau? su?
114. ə`θa`dɛga' lau? thwɛ?
115. ŋa' lu θu' θɛ?θe
116. θə`kho də`yo `kaŋ
117. koga' `cu `dudauŋ məyouŋya'`bu
118. cuŋ youŋ təphɛ? `kaŋ `θaðə`mi youŋ zouŋ`louŋ `kaŋ
119. luyouŋ θa? θe
120. `cə cha'hma' dəbya'`hmaŋ θi'
121. mwe`bwe khəbai? pai?
122. əyei? khogo əkhɛ? `cho`jo
123. θəyebə ei? θəye`na `sa

124. ʻsaˋbi khwɛˀ hmauˀ
125. ŋa ʻmwedɛʻmyauˀ ŋaˋgo chauˀ
126. təθɛˀʻlouŋ ʻsagɛʻðəhmyaʼ θaŋbəya təˋchaŋnɛʼ ce
127. nəbeiŋ thu lu khweʼ
128. myɛˀhna ʻhlwɛ ʻgɛ pyiˀ
129. chi hnəˋchauŋʻlɛ məkɛnɛʼ ʻmiŋ hle ʻmyɔˋlɛ məshɛnɛʼ
130. ʻceˋzu ʻkaŋ ʻlaŋ məmyiŋ
131. ʻgɛ hmaŋʻbudɛʼ saθəŋɛ
132. təkha ϑeˋbu pyiŋboʼ ʻna lɛ
133. ʻogo phɛʼyiŋ iŋgo phɛʼmɛ
134. ʻpa kaiˀ ʻna kaiˀ
135. θaŋgo cwɛˀ ʻsa ʻθago suŋ chi
136. kəˋla mənaiŋ yəkhaiŋ ʻmɛ
137. cwɛˀ mənaiŋloʼ ci ʻmi ʃoʼ
138. məˋsayaʼdɛʼ əˋmɛ ʻθɛnɛʼ pɛˀ
139. θuʼgo ŋa phyɛˀ ŋayiŋ pyɛˀ
140. yaŋgo yaŋˋjiŋ mətouŋˀʻhlyiŋnɛʼ
141. yaŋzaʼgo toze chiˀsaʼgo ʃeze
142. θiˀpiŋ auˀ coʼðɔ kogo piʼ lu auˀ coʼðɔ kogo məpiʼ
143. ʻca məˋyɛ tiˀ lu məˋyɛ hiˀ
144. cauˀtaˀ wuŋ ʻkiŋ
145. cauˀyweʼ məθe ʃɛˀyweʼ θe
146. pəˋshojouŋʻdɛgaʼ lɛˀʻθi pyaʼ
147. ʻca θehmaʼ luˋzuŋʻgauŋ pɔ
148. θəˋkho ʻpyehmaʼ ʻthoˋgwiŋ thaʼ
149. məˋyɛˋbɛ ʻcwɛˋbyɛ ʻsijiŋ
150. shiŋbyudɔ myɛˀhna shiŋˋmɛ məciʼwuŋʼ
151. cauˀyiŋ ʻlwɛ ʻyɛ ʻmiŋ phyiˀ
152. caʼ myeˋji tɛˀ ʃweˋthi
153. ʻyɛðɔ məθe θeðɔ ŋəˋyɛ məˋla
154. məˋyɛgəʼdɛ ʻpyeˋgɛze
155. zaməyiˋmyo əˋmwe təˋchauŋ əcuˀ məkhaŋ

156. təyauˀ ˋkauŋ təˋθauŋ boje nyɛˀnyɛˀ ce
157. ˋcauŋ ne ca shəyago məyoðe
158. gatha luˋdaiŋ ˋpe ˋte phyiˀ
159. ŋəˋyɛga′ lu pyabu məcauˀ
160. ywaˋnaga′myɛˀ ywaˋnwa məˋsa
161. təŋa miˊˋjauŋo məˋle
162. myiŋbaŋ ˋmyadɔ′ ŋɛ ˋnaŋbaŋ ˋmyadɔ′ pyɛ
163. hauŋˋluŋdɛ′ ˋkhwe lu məˋle
164. myɛˀhna θiˊ ŋəpi′ məwɛya
165. cauŋ o cwɛˀ məˋle
166. ˋkhwe oˋji ʃiˊˋkho θiŋlo′ mətaˀ
167. nəbyo θaŋhla′ nəo pauŋ ˋcoðəlauˀ ʃiˊ
168. nəo myɛˀnuˊ caiˀ
169. θəˋma oze ʃe′ne pyoze
170. təhleˋdɛ ˋsi təkhəˋyiˋdɛ ˋθwa
171. ˋe ətu pu əhyma′
172. ˋnɛyiŋ əŋa′ ˋmyayiŋ əwa′
173. ˋkauŋyiŋ saŋ ˋshoyiŋ hlaŋ
174. ŋəyaŋ′ ya′ ətudu ŋəkhu ya′ ˋkhwɛˋjaŋ ˋkhwɛˋjaŋ
175. ˋcigo bouˀ yoðe bouˀko ˋci yoðe
176. caŋ ða əsiŋ choðɛ lu əsiŋ məcho
177. cɛˀθuŋˋji ne əˋkauŋˋða ŋəyouˀˋθinɛ′ ˋpauŋhma′ əˋthauŋ
      khaŋya′
178. ŋəˋkhouŋma′ dəgauŋjauŋ′ təhleˋlouŋ pouˀ
179. ˋciˋgaŋ dəgauŋjauŋ′ ˋci əˋmya pyɛˀˋsiya′dɛ
180. təŋaˋna ˋni təŋa mouˀˋshoˋna ˋni mouˀˋsho
181. ˋgonena′ ˋgɔˋnɔ θamənena′ θaməˋnɔ
182. ˋmɛnɛ′ niˋba ətu ˋtha niˋba ˋmɛzɔ naŋ
183. θudɔˋjiŋˋjiŋ θəˋdiŋ lweˋlwe′ ˋpauŋbɛˀ twe′
184. seiˀ ˋpauŋ ko khwa
185. ʃeyiŋ shɛˀ toyiŋ phyaˀ
186. ˋnwa ˋkwɛ ˋca kaiˀ

187. θəˋkhwa ˋθihmaˊ əˋyi təjiŋ

188. khiŋya shweˋmyo meiŋya ˋhiŋˋgauŋ

189. əˋye ˋcigaˊ ˋθwe ˋniya

190. əmaˊ ˋkauŋˋza mauŋ ˋmyiŋ təlulu mauŋ ˋkauŋˋza əmaˊ
     ˋmibojauŋ

191. θiˀ təbiŋ ˋkauŋ hŋɛˀ təˋθauŋ ˋnanaiŋdɛ

192. ˋoˋjiŋ ˋtha ˋoˋjiŋ thiˊ ˋcoˋjiŋ ˋtha ˋcoˋjiŋ nyiˊ

193. chiŋˋðinɛˊ ˋsha ətu ˋtha ʃaˋbya paiŋbaiŋ mənenaiŋ

194. ˋθijeiŋ taŋ ˋθi pwiŋˊjeiŋ taŋ pwiŋˊ

195. nəˋphuza ywa lɛ

196. ˋʃaŋ caiˀ ˋnwa ˋchɔ ko thiŋ kədiŋ ʃweˋnaŋ

197. ko hniˀθɛˀkaˊ ˋthaŋbəlaˀ naˀyouˀ thiŋ

198. ŋɛyiŋ chiyaˊhmaˊ ˋciyiŋ hmiyaˊhmaˊ

199. pheiˀˋchiŋ pheiˀ eiˀˋthɛhma pheiˀ

200. shweˋjiŋ chouŋ louŋ ˋmyoˋjiŋ thaˀ myaˀ

201. seiˀ tu təθɛˀ mweˊ seiˀ mətu təθɛˀ meˊ

202. ŋɛgaˊ chiˀ əhniˀ təya məmeˊða ŋɛgaˊ ˋpauŋ əhniˀ təˋθauŋ
     məmeˊzəˋgauŋ

203. ŋəˋzeiŋ myiŋ ŋəgiŋ pyiˀ

204. eiŋʃeˊ pudɔˊ eiŋnauˀ məˋchaŋða

205. eiŋ θahmaˊ ɛˊ la

206. ˋda ˋtouŋˋdouŋnɛˊ wəˋlouŋ khouˀ

207. nəˋkhaŋbɛˋˋjiŋ ˋmi hmouˀ

208. dəbiŋ ˋlɛmu dəbiŋ thu

209. liŋnɛˊ məˋya ʃanɛˊ ˋθwa

210. ˋkaiŋ ˋcuŋ hmi ˋcuŋ ˋkaiŋ hmi

211. məˋya nezaˊ cauŋ θehmaˊ

212. ˋnwanɛˊ məˋya məθəˋnanɛˊ

213. ˋmi ˋwe cheiˀ ma

214. ˋsazəyadwiŋ əˋsa khɛˀ ˋthazəyadwiŋ məˋya khɛˀ

215. məˋyago chiˀ θegahmaˊ ˋchiˋmuŋyaˊmɛ

216. ˋpyɔbaŋ ˋmya məˋya zəˋga auŋ

217. maʹbɛˀ laiˀ maiˀphɛˀ pa

218. ʽshunɛʹ phɛˀlo ʽshu caʹ phɛˀ pauˀ phɛˀ caʹ phɛˀ pauˀ

219. kouŋ ʽʃouŋyiŋ təkhauˀ liŋgouŋ ʽʃouŋyiŋ təθɛˀʽlouŋ hmauˀ

220. ʽkhwelo liŋ məciŋnɛʹ

221. ʽθouŋʽjauŋ ʽpyauŋʽðə ʃiŋ ʽθouŋliŋ ʽpyauŋʽðə ʽmeiŋmaʹ

222. ye myiŋʹhmaʹ ca tiŋʹ

223. shwe ʽkauŋyiŋ dəzələ ʽmyo cwɛyiŋ dəzəʽlauŋ liŋ ʽkauŋhmaʹ
saŋyaʹ

224. pouˀbasəriʹyaʹ miʹnɛʹbaʹ

225. ʽθaðəʽmi məʽkauŋ miʹbaʹ ʽgauŋ

226. shiŋ ʽsiywe ʽmyiŋ yaŋda myiŋjiŋdɛ shiŋ ʽniŋywe ʽmyiŋ
kaŋda məmyiŋjiŋ

227. ʽtauŋʽzo pəʹlouŋʽzogoða pyiˀyaʹmɛ ʽθaʽzo θəʽmiʽzogo
məpyiˀyaʹ

228. gəba ʽmi lauŋ ʽθagauŋ chaʹ ʽniŋ

229. ko məchiʹ əmiʹðəʽlɛ ʽθa təʽgɛ

230. ʽnwaməʽdaŋ ʽθa məkhiŋ

231. θəʽu ʽyu

232. ʽwuŋnɛʹ məlwe ʽθa məmɛ ŋwenɛʹ məwɛ cuŋ məmɛ

233. miʹbaʹ zəʽga ʽna thauŋʽnya θaŋʽbya cauˀʽsauŋ coðə
ʽpyauŋ

234. ʽcwedouŋ ʽcwehlɛʹ ʽmwedouŋ ʽmwehlɛʹ

235. ʽθaʽgauŋ təyauˀ cauˀʽkauŋ dəziʹ

236. maʹ təthauŋ dəgauŋ ʽphwa

237. əbaʹ khwaya ʽtaiŋ

238. yaʹðayiŋ baʹ nəʽphu θaiˀ ʽtuyɛʹ

239. θəʽmi dəgauŋ ʽnwa təthauŋ

240. əmiʹ mɛʹʽθa ye ʽnɛ ʽŋa

241. shəya hmaŋyiŋ əlaŋ məsaiˀnɛʹ

242. ŋəpiʹ phouˀkohmaʹ shəya məpyaʹ ʽni məcaʹ

243. dəbɛʹ məʽkauŋ shəyaʹʽgauŋ

244. ʽchiʽmuŋ təbɛʹ kɛʹyɛʹ shəya

245. dəbɛʹ hnya yiŋ na

246. shəyago maŋ khu'ywe' ouʔ'khɛ əthu' khaŋya'dɛ
247. shəyadɛʔ dəbɛ' lɛʔ'sauŋ məthɛʔ
248. shəyago luŋðə 'yudɛ 'myiŋgo luŋðə 'mudɛ
249. kaŋðahlyiŋ əmi' kaŋðahlyiŋ əpha'
250. θegaŋ məyauʔ θɛʔ məpyauʔ
251. kaŋ məʃi' nyaŋ ʃi'ʹdaiŋ 'mwɛ
252. kaŋ cəma le shauŋhlyiŋ cauʔtauŋ`ji lwiŋ'ya'
253. kaŋ`zoma' 'θwaleyaya 'mo laiʔlo' ywa
254. ə`cauŋ tə tauŋbə ye 'si
255. nauŋga la nauŋga`ze pauʔyanɛ' 'yauŋ
256. naʔ 'thwiŋdɛ' gə`dwiŋ lu 'thwiŋdɛ' gə`dwiŋ məhouʔ
257. kaŋ 'kauŋdɛ' 'ca 'pye'yiŋ θəmiŋ twe'
258. əcheiŋ taŋdo' nəbeiŋ kaŋleiŋ'mɛ
259. məywɛ`bɛ sə`kɛ 'miŋ phyiʔ
260. ludaŋ kaŋ cha'
261. kaŋ youŋlo' 'shubouŋ mə`niŋnɛ'
262. 'ca'yɛya cəma mə`yoya
263. ouʔsa kaŋ sauŋ' əθɛʔ nyaŋ sauŋ'
264. 'shiŋ`yɛ təkha 'chaŋða təhlɛ'
265. ye`zi təkha yeða təhlɛ'
266. hmaŋ`giŋ təhlɛ' 'thiŋ təhlɛ'
267. youŋ 'cuji 'khwe 'cuji
268. θiʔŋouʔ myiŋ'douŋ myɛʔ myiŋ'douŋ
269. ne`ðeðəba' chouŋ`dɛga' jo 'θweðəba' təmya'mya'
270. əyeiʔ la nebuga' sauŋ'ya'
271. əmauŋ`lɛ yauʔ ŋa'ʹnwa`lɛ pyauʔ
272. 'thaŋ`ði cwegaiʔ 'ci 'niŋlaiʔ
273. ŋojiŋyɛʔ lɛʔ to'
274. cɛʔ'kaŋ shaŋ`o 'to
275. khə`yaŋ`ði peiŋgaiʔ 'da 'touŋgaiʔ
276. ye ŋaʔθu ye`dwin`dɛ ca'
277. 'kuŋ`ði caiʔ tauŋŋu po'

278. sula′ leiꜘ ye cha′

279. mi′ꜛjauŋgo yehma hluꜘ

280. ꜛkhwe o θəye′jonɛ′ chi

281. ꜛsaya′gaŋ couŋ mouꜘsheiꜘ ꜛpya ꜛswɛ

282. θəꜛkhogo taiꜘꜛso ꜛhniŋ ꜛsouŋgo ꜛθa kiŋ ꜛkhaiŋ

283. θəꜛkho ʃi′ya wuŋdouꜘ wuŋꜛbonɛ′ ꜛθwa

284. təkhulaꜘko ʃa təliŋgwago twe′

285. khaꜘpyago ʃwe hmaꜘlo′ paŋmi′

286. daꜘtə hmaꜘlo′ kəlaꜘpɔ tiŋ ꜛkogwɛba kəlaꜘpɔ ca′hma′
    kəleiŋzi′ꜛhmaŋ θi′

287. phə′ya hmaꜘlo′ ꜛkogwɛba phuꜘ thwɛꜘhma′ tauŋbo′ꜛhmaŋ
    θi′

288. chiꜘꜛti hmaꜘlo′ ꜛpe′zaba ꜛmo′liŋhma′ ꜛphoθudə′hmaŋ θi′

289. ŋa′θə′mi leiŋmahla′ðihu′ ꜛchi′muŋnegaiꜘ yauꜘma′ ꜛmyiŋ
    ꜛsi thwɛꜘ

290. thaiŋne ə′kauŋꜛða tha′ꜛðwahma′ ꜛco′hmaŋ θi′

291. ꜛŋadaꜘ ꜛcauŋdəga ꜛcauŋdəganɛ′ ə′shouŋ θaꜘtə′ ꜛŋadaꜘ
    khiŋ′ji əlaŋ′ʃubagə′la

292. shiŋ′bodɛꜘ ꜛchuŋ′bo ꜛci

293. ku′ðo də′bɛ ŋə′yɛ dəbeiꜘθa

294. cɛꜘ naywe′ ꜛhu′ya ꜛme ꜛcwɛgo θaꜘ tiŋ

295. cɛꜘu′byouꜘ θaŋdouꜘnɛꜘ cha′

296. cwɛꜘ nəywɛꜘ wɛꜘhma taꜘ

297. khin′jinɛ′ ꜛbi əkwa′ji

298. gə′dauŋjaiꜘ tə′lwɛ phiŋ tə′lwɛ

299. khouꜘya tə′cha ʃa′ya tə′cha

300. nyauŋ ꜛu ꜛkaŋ′ba pyo saŋpanəgoga′ nəma′ ꜛkha ꜛco

301. ꜛpwɛ məci′ꜛbɛnɛ′ saŋpa′ lu ꜛto khaŋya′

302. chi′jo ꜛthaŋ tɛꜘ əchɛꜘ məca′

303. hlɔ′ga wuŋ tiŋ

304. səpho ouꜘko ʃwe θouꜘ si

305. seiŋ cauꜘ ꜛyauŋya ꜛshe′yoðɛga′ kaŋ′laŋ′

306. ꜛmyiŋ′gauŋ ꜛpyeya ꜛkhwe′jo kaŋ′laŋ′

307. ˋshuŋzaŋˋdɛ cwɛˀˋchi ˋyɔ

308. bəzaˀka′ phəˋya phəˋya lɛˀka′ ˋkaˋya ˋkaˋya

309. phauŋ ˋsiyɛˀ ye ŋaˀ

310. lɛ thuŋ ˋθwa ˋnwa me′

311. ŋo ˋadɛˀ yi ˋa θaŋ

312. əba′dɛˀ ˋθa təla′ ˋci

313. ˋnwa ʃe′ thuŋ ˋcu

314. tauŋya ʃiŋgo myauˀ laiˀ

315. θəˋkhoga′ lu lu hiˀ

316. nauˀ eiˀ əyiŋ pyɔ

317. nauˀhma′ kiŋ əyiŋ cɛˀtɛ′ ˋpha

318. nauˀhma′ ˋmwe mi′ ˋu hmɛ′jiŋ

319. bədeiŋ mətaˀkhiŋ ʃweˋgo θiŋ

320. məthaiŋgiŋ chi ˋshiŋ

321. youŋ məya′giŋ θaŋbəya ʃa

322. ʃiŋ məpyu′giŋga′ lu thwɛˀ chiŋ

323. ˋhiŋjo məˋmyiya′giŋ hnouˀˋθi ˋsihniŋ′dɛ

324. əme cɔ ˋdwedɔ ˋluŋ

325. pəˋsho məʃi′ðuga′ louŋauŋ thaiŋ ˋpyɔ

326. chilyiŋ kɛba ˋmyiŋðəˋma

327. theiˀko pouˀˋpihma′ kədɔ′

328. dəbɛ′ ʃa shəya twe′

329. sauŋˋgauŋgo ʃa phəlaŋbiŋgo twe′

330. məpoˋˋbɛnɛ′ ˋmɛza yauˀ

331. əˋco lolo′ nyauŋye ˋlauŋ paˀˋthaŋ twe′

332. ˋbədi′biŋ ˋpyolo′ pauŋ ˋco

333. nyauŋ ˋcholo′ ʃwe ˋo ya′

334. pɔ′zelolo′ cauŋyouˀ ˋtho ˋshe ətwɛˀ ˋle

335. myɛˀmyɛˀ ˋsajiŋlo′ ˋshaiŋˋdɛ laiˀ ˋhnɛˋji ˋniŋmi′lo′ ŋwe ˋŋajaˀ yɔya′

336. əˋe caiˀtɛ′ lugo nebuhma ˋhlaŋ

337. saiŋ kɔlo′ chouŋbɔ yauˀ

338. ˋcaˊmi ˋshwɛmiˊðəlo hluˀyaˊhmaˋlɛ khɛˀ ˋshwɛˋthayaˊ-
hmaˋlɛ khɛˀ

339. bəˋdaiŋˋðilo shouˀyiŋˋlɛ ˋsu ˋsayiŋˋlɛ ˋyu

340. ʃeˊ ˋto dəˋbo nauˀ shouˀ ˋhlɛdouˀ

341. ˋsayaˊhmaˋlɛ ˋθɛnɛˊ ʃaˀʃaˀ pyiˀyaˊhmaˋlɛ əshinɛˊ ˋywɛˋywɛ

342. ˋpezəyaˋlɛ ŋwe məʃiˊ ˋpyezəyaˋlɛ mye məʃiˊ

343. louˀ ˋsa ˋmokhauŋ ˋkho ˋsa ˋkhwe hauŋ

344. baˊˋjigoˋlɛ mətweˊ ˋthi tiŋˋbwɛgoˋlɛ məhmi

345. phuˀ məyaˊ dəmaˊ ˋshouŋ

346. hle ˋpyeˋdouŋ tɛˀ ˋco

347. əˋye ˋkauŋ ˋdeiŋˋdauŋ phyɛˀ

348. əyiŋ ˋphouŋˋji təchɛˀ khauˀ nauˀ ˋphouŋˋji hnəchɛˀ khauˀ

349. nauˀ ladɛˊ mauŋ pəˋlɛ ˋdaiŋwuŋdɛˀ ˋkɛ

350. təˋmiŋ ˋlɛhmaˊ təˋmiŋ əˋcogo θiˊ

351. phuˀ miˊˋjauŋ phyiˀ myiˀ məˋchaŋða

352. ˋca cauˀloˊ ʃiŋˋji ˋko ʃiŋˋji ˋcadɛˀ ˋsho

353. ənabədwiŋ əna shiŋˊ

354. gəba ˋmi lauŋ shiˋmigwɛˀ thaˊ tauˀ

355. nuya ˋwɛ ˋswɛ

356. mwe puya ˋkiŋ hmauŋˊ

357. ˋbu ˋlɛya phəyouŋ shiŋˊ

358. phuˀ ˋminˋða pya yəˋtha shaiˀ

359. ʃiŋ ˋnɛloˊ ˋshiˋbuba ɛˀgaˊ lu thwɛˀ

360. ˋmi lauŋya le piŋˊ

361. ˋeðugo ye ku puðugo ˋmi taiˀ

362. ˋlɛya θəˋkho ˋthauŋ

363. mye neiŋˊya hlaŋ saiˀ

364. ye niˀθu ˋwa kuloˊ ˋtho

365. yeˋga neiŋˊyaðoˊ ˋsiði

366. myɛˀhna ˋciya ˋhiŋbaˀ pa

367. θəˋthe ˋce paŋˊ

368. cauˀpadɛ sho cauŋnɛˊ toˊ

369. caŋgo wɛ souʔpa sho ʽpeiŋ uʹgo wɛ ʽsa

370. əʽpaʽjiŋ tweʹdɔʹ lɛʽbiŋ pyaʔ

371. gəʽdouŋbɔ theiʔ kwɛʔ

372. mweʽbwe ʽpo thiʹ

373. θəʽkholɛʔ θəwɛʔ luʹ

374. θəmouʔdəya ʽwuŋ təthwa

375. təneʹ chuʔ təlaʹ muʔ

376. kəʹla khaʔθiʹ ye kəʹla ʽθouŋyweʹ məlauʔ

377. lu ʽshiŋʽyɛ təeiŋdauŋgo lu ʽchaŋða shɛeiŋdauŋ ʽpeloʹ
     məlauʔ

378. ouʔsago phyo səphogaʹ

379. ʽsidɛʹ ye shɛdɛʹ gəʽziŋ

380. eiʔ pauʔnɛʹ ʽpha kauʔ

381. θəmiŋ ʽmweʽyiŋ ʽca ʽsaʽyiŋ

382. dəʽbɛdaŋjauŋʹ təʽkhwedaŋ pyɛʔ

383. təʽyauʔmaʹgo myiŋ təʽodaŋ pyɛʔ

384. shiŋbyudɔ wiŋmɛʹha chi dəbiŋnɛʹ ʽceiŋ ce

385. wuŋnɛʹ ʽa ʽlenɛʹ ʽhmya

386. ʽcwe tiŋ ʃiŋbəyiŋ shaʔmɛ

387. ʃiʹ cauŋʹjaʹ məʃiʹ tauŋʹdaʹ

388. ʽca ʽci chiya ʽci

389. ʽkiŋchiʽmya chi təʽchauŋ ʽcoyweʹ əʽθwa məpyɛʔ

390. shiŋ couŋ ʽcwɛ

391. hŋɛʔ məyaʹgiŋ ʃiŋʹ ʃa

392. θiʔ məyaʹgiŋ ʽwa ʽpauŋ kuʔ

393. ʽmo ywaʽdouŋ ye khaŋ

394. laʹ θaʽdouŋ ʽbaiŋ ŋiŋ

395. ʽŋa luŋhmaʹ kuŋ pyiʔ

396. ʽmo θauʔ cɛʔ tiŋ ne wiŋ zəʽba ʽhlaŋ

397. ʽmogo liŋʹyweʹ ʽpyo yiŋʹði

398. ywa luŋhmaʹ ywɛʔ taiʔ

399. siʔ məyauʔkhiŋ ʽhmya kouŋ

400. siˀ yauˀhma' `hmya chuŋ

401. shiŋ laiˀhma' θiˀpiŋ ʃa

402. lumaiˀ nauˀhma' əcaŋ ya'

403. khaˀ`kwiŋ pyiŋdanɛ' ywaðiˀ`ci yauˀ

404. `chi yo jo `θweneya'danɛ' ŋəni`ji `piyɔ'

405. ʃiŋbəyiŋ təkha thwɛˀ `pɛ`ji təhle cɛˀ

406. ŋouˀmi' `θɛdaiŋ tɛˀnaiŋ `phya yauˀ

407. təne' təlaŋ pəgaŋ bɛ ywe'mə`lɛ

408. suˀ`pidɛ' lɛˀko məchauˀpazenɛ'

409. khu' ye`dwin `tu khu' yeji θauˀchiŋ

410. khu' liŋ ne khu' `θa `mwejiŋ

411. `ŋa pwɛˀya ŋə`hmya laiˀcha'

412. ə`phya tɛˀ əhmɛ' `saya'`no`no

413. gəduˀpauˀka' `byaiŋ sauŋ'

414. di youŋ myiŋlo' di chouŋ thwiŋdɛ

415. hnyɔða hnyɔ ŋəjɔ mə`saya'

416. yauˀkhəma' θe`hmaŋ məθi' `myiŋ wɛ mə`siya'`la

417. ə`θa lo ə`yo `tauŋ

418. le shiŋgo ci'ywe' ywɛˀ taiˀ

419. mu'`ða məpa liŋga mə`chɔ

420. wiŋ wiŋ `jiŋ shauˀnɛ' `thwiŋ

421. ə`caŋ hmu' ənu'phyiŋ'ða auŋzeya

422. əna khaŋhma' əθa saŋya'

423. `su neya `su shauˀ neya shauˀ

424. aˀnɛ' `thwiŋywe' phyiˀlauˀθi' əyago pauˀsheiŋnɛ'
      məpauˀθa

425. shiŋ chi`ðɔ `conɛ' cɛˀ chiðɔ mə`myɛ cɛˀ chi`ðɔ `conɛ' **shiŋ**
      chiðɔ məkhaŋnaiŋ

426. sa u' `dauŋ ouˀ `dauŋ u' sa ouˀ

427. kuŋ `leði ˀ`kwiŋnɛ' ŋə`ziŋgo ouˀywe' məmi'naiŋ kuŋ
      lɛˀ`leðiˀnɛ' `ŋa`ji pyiˀlo' məya'naiŋ

428. chiŋðe'zi θeiŋgi ʃwegwɛˀhma `nadɛ

B.P.—H

429. gəlouŋ pye gəlouŋ nə'ga pye nə'ga

430. 'cuŋciŋya leiŋma

431. ə'mya 'mo'ga ye θauʔ

432. 'mo pyo ə'mya 'ni

433. θaŋga 'a phə'ya məshaŋnaiŋ

434. 'mi 'ci 'mi naiŋ ye 'ci ye naiŋ

435. 'a mətaŋ maŋ ʃɔ'

436. 'khwe 'yu phɛʔ kaiʔ 'khwe'gauŋ nəywɛʔ pyaʔ

437. ə'sa mətɔðɔ təlouʔ ə'θwa mətɔðɔ tə'hlaŋ

438. caʃe 'wamɛ' 'θwa ə'yo ci' ʃauŋ

439. 'khwego yaiʔchiŋgə'dɛ 'khweʃiŋ myɛʔhna thauʔya'^ðe

440. məchiʔθɔ'lɛ auŋ'ga 'naŋ mə'naŋðɔ'lɛ piŋ'ðɛʔ ʃu

441. luleiŋma əmyɛʔ pyiŋ məthwɛʔ

442. θi'ða θi'ze məmyiŋzenɛ'

443. ɛ'ðɛ nyiŋ'nɛʔ əeiʔ khɛʔ

444. ɛ'ðɛ əθɛʔ khuŋnəyɛʔ

445. məkhɔ'bɛ mə'θwanɛ' mətɔ'bɛ mə'sanɛ'

446. nya' 'pyɔ auʔ ci' ne' 'pyɔ nauʔ ci'

447. 'tɔzə'ga 'tɔhma pyauʔ

448. teiʔteiʔ ne thauŋ taŋ

449. 'bu tə'louŋ shauŋ oauŋ mə'shiŋ'yɛ'bu

450. ko cuŋyiŋ hnouʔlo' ya'naiŋdɛ zə'ga cuŋyiŋ hnouʔlo'
     məya'naiŋ

451. məlyɔ' mə'tiŋ 'sauŋ'jo 'hnyiŋ

452. taŋyiŋ 'she luŋyiŋ 'be

453. əchiʔ 'ciyiŋ əmyɛʔ 'cidɛ

454. piŋnya luŋðɔ zaga' wi'ri'ya' luŋðɔ ouʔdeiʔsa' θəda luŋðɔ
     yaga'

455. əwuʔ luŋðɔ i'na' ə'θouŋ luŋθɔ daθa' ə'sa luŋðɔ bəya' əeiʔ
     luŋðɔ 'mɔha'

456. zə'ga luŋ cuŋ phyiʔ

457. sedəna luŋ cuŋ phyiʔ

458. hnə`louŋ `kauŋ wuŋ `ci

459. shəya `mya `θa θe

460. ŋə`θaiŋ `mya `hiŋ houŋ

461. zə`ga `mya ə`hma pa

462. zə`ga zə`ga `pyɔbaŋ `mya zə`ga`dɛga´ zati´ pya´

463. ə`twe nɛʔyiŋ ə`ye pyɛʔ

464. ci`za θaŋ yaŋ

465. `khwebu´ yaŋ lo lubu´ seiʔ to hledo pɛ´ khɛʔ

466. əlo `ci əya´ `ni

467. aʔ wiŋ pauʔsheiŋ thwɛʔ

468. mə`sayɛʔ lauʔ tɛʔ

469. `ləba´ `ciðu zə`ga cho

470. əkuʔ məʃi´dɛ´ `caŋ bə`yaŋbəda

471. ə`theiŋ məʃi´dɛ´ chigiŋ

472. cauŋ məʃi´lo´ cwɛʔ `myu

473. `tɔ `mi lauŋ `təjauŋ lɛʔ`paŋbauʔ khaʔ

474. khiŋ`ji lɛʔ`yaŋ tɛʔka´ mauŋyiŋ caʔ`khoziŋ mətɛʔ`la

475. khauŋga´ `mo yo

476. əhmaiʔka´ sa´ pya´θaʔ `mi lauŋ

477. `pya dəzɛʔcauŋ´ pye pyɛʔ

478. əpyɛʔ əpyɛʔnɛ´ hnə`khauŋ`ðwe thwɛʔ

479. yedeiŋ niʔ

480. cauŋ `θwaywe´ `shi`hniŋ məcwe

481. `khwe`hle khouŋlo´ phouŋ mətha´

482. `khwe hauŋlo´ tauŋbo´ mə`pye

483. sagə`le təsheiʔsajauŋ´ mye `ɔza məphyiʔhnaiŋ

484. `hnaŋ dəzi´nɛ´ shi məphyiʔhnaiŋ

485. `nwa khəlauʔ myibedɛ´ `hnaŋ məya´

486. shiŋwuŋgədə əcauŋ´ja´ məhouʔ

487. `oga´ məpu sə`lauŋga´ pu

488. `myiŋga´ məhlouʔ khouŋdaiŋga´ hlouʔ

489. youŋ ətwɛʔ chouŋga´ cauŋ´ja´

490. kauʔˋhnyiŋgaˊ məˋsi shaŋˋjaŋgaˊ ˋsi
491. ˋcwɛ hnəkauŋ khaʔtɛˊˋja myezabiŋ məkhaŋnaiŋ
492. cɛʔ zəˋba ˋsa thəyaŋ daŋ θiŋˊ
493. ˋtouŋgo ˋmoˋjo pyiʔ pouʔθiŋba hmaŋ
494. θiʔ hnəpiŋ saʔˋcagaˊ ˋwa
495. tauŋ ˋlɛyiŋ myɛʔ pyaʔ
496. ˋshuŋ khaŋˋyiŋ hŋɛʔ θiŋˊ

Suggestions for Further Reading

The Soul of a People, H. Fielding. Macmillan & Co. Ltd, London, 1898.

The Silken East, V. C. Scott O'Connor, Vols i & ii. Hutchinson, London, 1904.

Mandalay and Other Cities of the Past in Burma, V. C. Scott O'Connor. Hutchinson, London, 1907.

The Burman: his Life and Notions, Shway Yoe. Macmillan & Co. Ltd, London, 1910.

British Rule in Burma, 1824–1942, G. E. Harvey. Faber & Faber, London, 1946.

Burmese Family, Mi Mi Khaing. Longmans, Green & Co., London, 1946.

Burmese Folk-Tales, Htin Aung. O.U.P., 1948.

Handbook of Oriental History, edited by C. H. Phillips. The Royal Historical Society, London, 1951.

Burma under the Japanese, Thakin Nu, edited and translated with Introduction by J. S. Furnivall. Macmillan & Co. Ltd, London, 1954.

A History of South-East Asia, D. G. E. Hall. St Martin's Press Inc., New York, 1955.

The Union of Burma, A Study of the First Years of Independence, Hugh Tinker. O.U.P., 1957.

Burma in the Family of Nations, Dr Maung Maung. Djambatam, Amsterdam, 1958.

Perspective of Burma, 'The Atlantic', Vol. 201, No. 2. Concord, N.H., 1958.

My Burma, The Autobiography of a President, U Ba U. Taplinger Publishing Co. Inc., New York, 1959.

Burma, D. G. E. Hall. Hutchinson, London, 1960.

Abbreviations used in the Text

(The abbreviated titles are those given in the new *Burmese–English Dictionary*.)

B.E.D. *A Burmese English Dictionary*, published in parts by the School of Oriental and African Studies, London.

B.S.O.A.S. *Bulletin of the School of Oriental and African Studies*, London.

Hm. Yaz. *Hman-nam Yaza-win-daw-gyi*, i, ii, iii ('The Glass Palace Chronicle'). Mandalay, 1921, 1908, 1907.

J.B.R.S. *Journal of the Burma Research Society*.

Kandaw M. Com. *Kandaw Min-gyaung Myit-ta-za Hnin La-gaung A-phye* ('Religious and moral instruction') by Kandaw Min-gyaung Sa-ya-daw (15th c.), and commentary by Min-gyaung Sa-ya-daw (19th c.). Rangoon, 1925.

O.E.D. *Oxford English Dictionary*.

Sagab. *Sa-ga-bon Hna-htaung* (Two Thousand Burmese Proverbs), Sa-ya Taing (20th c.). Rangoon, 1910.

Sagab. B. *Sa-ga-bon Baung-gyok* (A Collection of Burmese Proverbs), Kyi-gan Shin-gyi (18th c.), Atu-la Sa-ya-daw (18th c.), Shin Thi-la-wun-tha (15th c.). Rangoon, 1902.

S.I.P. *Selections from the Inscriptions of Pagan, 12th–14th c.*, Pe Maung Tin and G. H. Luce. Rangoon, 1928.

Wisit. Link. Sagab. *Wi-sitra Lin-ga-ra Sa-ga-bon* (Moral instruction, proverbs and their origin), U Tha Hto. Rangoon, 1919.

Wisit. Por. Sagab. *Wi-sitra Porana Sa-ga-bon A-phye* (Proverbs and their origin). Rangoon, 1922.

Wisit. Sagab. *Myit-ta-za Amyo-myo Hnin Wi-sitra Sa-ga-bon Baung-gyok* (Anecdotes, model letters, etc.), Maung Tok. Mandalay, 1921.

Yazaw. K. *Ya-zaw-wa-da Kyan* (Moral instruction for kings), Mon-ywe Sa-ya-daw, A.D. 1832. Mandalay, 1926.

Various Sources

ENGLISH

The Birds of Burma, B. E. Smythies. London, 1953.

Burmese Drama, Maung Htin Aung. O.U.P., 1937.

Burmese Proverbs (MS.) in French, by Father Faure, a Roman Catholic missionary.

Dhammapāda Commentary, Buddhist Legends, etc. Three volumes, Harvard, 1921.

Government of Burma, *Burma Handbook*. Simla, 1943.

Hitopadesa, A new literal translation from the Sanskrit Text of Professor F. Johnson, by F. Pincott. London, 1880.

(The) Jātaka, or Stories of the Buddha's former births, edited by E. B. Cowell. C.U.P., Vols. I–VI, 1895–1907, and Vol. VII, Index, 1913.

Konmara Pya Zat, Introduction and Translation, Hla Pe. London, 1952.

Malay Proverbs, Sir Richard Winstedt. John Murray, London, 1950.

'On Siamese Proverbs and Idiomatic Expressions', Col. G. E. Gerini, from the *Journal of the Siam Society*, 1904.

Racial Proverbs, edited by S. G. Champion. George Routledge & Sons, Ltd, London, 1938.

BURMESE

Chwe-ta-gyin (Guide to Domestic Economy), U Kha. Prome (Burma)' 1931.

Hmaing We We Wutthu (fiction), Maung Khin Maung. Rangoon, 20th c.

Khin Myint Gyi Wutthu (fiction), i, ii, Maung Khin Maung. Rangoon, 1931, 1926.

Loka Nīti Pāt Nissaya (Translation of *Loka Nīti*), Mahā-wi-thok-dā-rama Sa-ya-daw. Rangoon, 1928.

Maung Hmaing Wutthu (fiction), i, iii, U Kyi. Rangoon, 1904, 1905.

Maung San Thu Ma Phwa Thaik Pon Wutthu (fiction), i, Sa-ya Saw. Rangoon, 1917.

Maung Ta Naw Wutthu (fiction), i, ii, Sa-ya Thin. Rangoon, 1906.

Mr Maung Hmaing Hma-daw-bon Wutthu (Miscellany), i, ii, iii, 'Mr Maung Hmaing'. Rangoon, 1925, 1928, 1921.

Sa-be-bin Wutthu (fiction), U Lat. Rangoon, 1931.

Sa-ga-bon Thon-daung (Three Thousand Proverbs), U Tun Kyaing. Rangoon, 1955.

Shwe-pyi-zo Wutthu (fiction), U Lat. Rangoon, 1929.

Ta-bin-Shwe-hti Wutthu-daw-gyi (Historical Novel) i, ii, iii, iv, Le-di Pan-di-ta U Maung Gyi. Rangoon, 20th c.

Tha-mi Lein-ma Ma-ha Shwe-thwe Wutthu (fiction), 'Met-ma-pye'. Rangoon, 20th c.

Than Than Wutthu (fiction), ii, iii, iv, Maung Khin Maung. Rangoon, 1920-1.

Thu-te-tha-na Tha-yok-pya Dictionary (encyclopaedia), Ashin Obhāsā-bhivamsa. Rangoon, 1955.

Tint Tint Khin Wutthu (fiction), 'Mandalay Ne La'. Rangoon, 1920.

Index to Words in the Proverbs

References are to the numbers of the proverbs. Not all the words are included in the Index, which is intended only to supplement the sectional headings given in the Contents.